FINN'S WORLD

Finn's World

Finn Ní Fhaoláin

GILL BOOKS

GILL BOOKS
Hume Avenue
Park West
Dublin 12
www.gillbooks.ie

Gill Books is an imprint of M.H. Gill & Co.

© Finn Ní Fhaoláin 2017
978 07171 7255 9

Designed by Graham Thew
Photography by Leo Byrne
Food and props styling by Jette Virdi
Edited by Emma Dunne
Indexed by Eileen O'Neill
Printed by BZ Graf, Poland

PROPS
Created and Found by Jette Virdi www.createdandfound.com
Industry
Article
Irish Design Store

This book is typeset in Hoefler Titling Lt Roman 9pt.

The paper used in this book comes from the wood pulp of
managed forests. For every tree felled, at least one tree is
planted, thereby renewing natural resources.

Dedicated to my wonderful nanas,
Georgina and Catherine, who
instilled in me from an early age a
passion for food and a zest for life.

Acknowledgements

I will be forever thankful to the amazing Marianne Gunn O'Connor and Nicki Howard for taking a chance on me. Deirdre Nolan for everything; having a fellow excited coeliac onboard was a joy I could never have expected. Sarah Liddy for graciously showing me the ropes and Teresa Daly for embracing every bonkers idea I had. To Gráinne O'Reilly and Emma Lynam for all their enthusiasm, wonderful ideas and support along the way. Catherine Gough for her kind, encouraging notes and recipe testing. The whole Gill Books team for making a book that made me squeal the first time I saw it.

My family, specifically my parents, Val and Colum, my nanas, Catherine and Georgina, and my aunty, Katherine, for their support, encouragement and boundless enthusiasm for all my mad notions.

The wonderful gang on the cookbook shoots; I never knew work could be so much fun. Leo Byrne for his keen eye and patience with my inability to keep a straight face. Jette Virdi for her stunning work and ingenuity with my minimalist kitchen, and Aoife for her bright humour and wonderful cooking.

To all the amazing people and businesses who supported the shoot up in Bundoran: Aranxta of ID Languages, Fiona of Whitehill Eco Farm, Sean of Tolan Projects, Sian of Flotsam & Jetsam Coffee, and all at Turf n' Surf Hostel and Bundoran Surf Co. for putting up the crew and hosting our BBQ. Huib for putting a soundtrack to my cooking and my Surfworld family for all their encouragement.

To the Fáilte Ireland Culinary Course and Saint Angela's College, Sligo. Hats off to Eithna O'Sullivan, Brid Torrades, Amanda McCloat and all the ladies who kept us going in the kitchen those ten weeks on Lough Gill.

To Fiona Hallinan, who may not have realised it at the time, but who was the catalyst for my culinary career and has been a tremendous support ever since.

Thank you to Dawn and Keith in Marbella for the well-needed rest before the whole adventure began. To Cian Brassil, my tech guru and surf inspiration. To my mermaids, Gráinne, Fiona and Aoife, without whom my love of the sea would have been a lonely place. Louise and Eamonn, my No. 1 fans since day one. Eavan and Callum for not being bored to tears when I constantly talked about my business. Sandy in the Gyreum for the best kitchen chats. To the boys at Grown Clothing, who've been there since the start. To Deirdre McGloin and all my ACORNS ladies, who held me up when I started to flag. Susan Jane White and Katie Jane Sanderson, who have been my foodie crushes since I fell down the rabbit hole of culinary exploration. Thank you to the wonderful folk I spent time with in Tenerife while writing up the manuscript: that island of sunshine, blue seas and delicious food will live in my heart forever.

About the Author

Finn Ní Fhaoláin was born in Ireland to an
author mother and filmmaker father. By the age
of ten she had already sailed past a glacier in
Alaska, stayed in a convent in the south of France
and watched cobras dance in India. She has a
bachelor's degree in Earth and Ocean Science and
a master's degree in Marine Biology. Her mission
– which she had to accept as a broke student
diagnosed as a coeliac – is to prove that you can
have delicious, healthy food that is also cheap and
easy to prepare. She lives, surfs and cooks in a
seaside town on the northwest coast of Ireland.

Contents

Introd

uction

Where I Am

Over the past few years I've begun to understand how a healthy life fits together. I've no idea why when I was younger I couldn't see how the food I ate affected how I performed in sports, how the fuel you put in affects the performance of the machine. It took me a longer time still to see this on a bigger scale. Your whole lifestyle – where you live, what you eat, what you do, how you exercise and the people you surround yourself with – has to work together to make a happy, healthy human.

In the winter of 2015, I was living on the east coast of Ireland and feeling first-hand what it's like when you don't have these aspects in balance. Though I was fairly pleased with myself at the time – I had set up as a sole trader, I was writing this book and I was doing some work with a really cool restaurant in Dublin – I felt lonely, frustrated and unfulfilled.

In terms of a balanced life, I had the food sorted (I was eating really well) and the exercise down (I was working with a personal trainer so I could get into competitive powerlifting) and I was doing work that I loved. But I still felt off – my friends were scattered across the country (I had gone to college in Galway and Cork) and I was back living at home for the first time since before college. I was sitting there in my mid-twenties with debt from a master's degree that I wasn't even using and getting up at obscene times to make the long commute into Dublin, and when I finished work I felt like I had no core group of friends to relax or go out with.

To top it all off, my favourite sport, passion, pastime – surfing – was totally off the cards, as there are no regular waves on the east coast! And while that might not sound like a big deal to some, it was a huge loss for me. I'm a water baby, plain and simple. I've generally never lived more than a mile or two from the sea. I studied ocean science and marine biology and I used to work in an aquarium. Some of my address names have included The Quays, Kinvarra, Crest of the Wave and Ocean Wave. Sure my name is Finn, for goodness sake!

It was time for a change.

Having gained confidence from my cooking and baking jobs, I started looking at culinary arts courses. A wonderful opportunity arose when I received a scholarship for a full culinary programme in St Angela's College in Sligo.

On the introductory day for the course I happened to sit next to a girl who lived in Bundoran. Bundoran is a little surfing town in the south of Donegal where I had spent a very happy summer living in a cottage and surfing while I wrote up my master's thesis. When I asked her if she was moving temporarily for the course, she pointed out that it was just 20 minutes from Bundoran to the culinary school. A massive flash went off in my mind – I swear it was like my brain did a flip.

I could live in a town I loved, with a wonderful community of people I already knew, and I could surf any time and go on hikes in the mountains, all while doing my course and writing my book. And I could afford to stay afterwards, as I wouldn't be dealing with Dublin commuter-belt rent prices. It's amazing how a few small choices can change your entire life. Fast forward a few months and life's set-up looks something like this: I've an apartment with an office and a beautiful kitchen that looks over one of Ireland's best-known reef breaks. I've no morning commute so my petrol gets saved for surf trips.

It's my first time living alone and I've never been less lonely. There's a wonderful, vibrant community in this little town on the wild Atlantic, many of whom have their own start-up businesses too. There's always someone keen to go for a surf, to a yoga class, for a hike up in the mountains or listen to some live music and grab a sneaky pint in one of the pubs.

On the foodie front I've lucked out with great food suppliers, local farms and craft butchers. Sligo town is not too far away for odder items and there are great beaches and woods nearby for foraging bits as well. I love cooking for friends in my little blue-and-white-tiled kitchen and during the summer months there are lots of barbecues and parties to cater for around the town. But why did I end up swapping a long-term career plan in marine science for food and going from an early college diet of pizza and cereal to healthy, home-cooked food?

How I Got Here

I'm a small, bubbly blonde with the energy levels of a Labrador and the sense of humour of a teenage boy. I was always a happy, active kid, swimming in the lake or sea, climbing trees and building forts, but there were also bouts of unexplained stomach problems and a shoddy immune system that led to regular colds and flus. I was brought to doctors, specialists, herbalists and homoeopaths. They had all sorts of answers: abdominal migraines, an imbalance in my gut flora, over-anxious personality ... maybe it was all in my head!

When I shipped off to college, things began to spiral downwards. My diet had been pretty healthy at home. There were never fizzy drinks or sweets in the house and, as my friends said, we ate a lot of 'weird food' i.e. tofu, falafel and unusual-looking vegetables. Now fending for myself in a student apartment, what I had been taught growing up didn't gel with the priorities of an 18-year-old who wanted to spend her money on sports gear and socialising.

I ate cereal for breakfast, toasties for lunch and for dinner I had pizza-eating competitions with my 6-foot-4 rugby-player housemate.

Wheat, wheat and more wheat!

My energy started to disappear, my stomach cramped uncontrollably whenever I ate, dark circles appeared

under my eyes and, sometimes, ulcers in my mouth. As I lost strength and weight, I gave up all the sports I loved so much and I started to look like a bobble-head doll on the dashboard of a car.

I went to my local GP, who suggested cutting out wheat and dairy. Being a vegetarian already, my food choices were now severely restricted. I started including more rye and barley in my diet.

I thought I was healthy, but I looked like death. The energy dips got worse. Eventually I couldn't carry a stack of plates up the stairs in the vegetarian restaurant where I was working: a far cry from the little girl who used to challenge her godfather to an arm wrestle and who could almost lift up her mum.

Something had to change. I went for a consultation at the Irish Institute of Nutrition and Health. A wonderful woman there connected with the kid inside me who used to put on Darina Allen-inspired cookery shows for Mum and Dad. I was given recipes for breads, protein bars and simple meals that cut out wheat, dairy and refined sugars. They were tasty but they couldn't replace the junk food I craved on the weekends.

When I snuck two slices of pizza one night, my stomach cramped so badly I could see the muscles moving. I returned to the doctor. It was suggested I might have Crohn's Disease. I freaked. (Never google any ailment, ever – it will convince you that you're going to die!)

I was put on a waiting list for scope tests. On the day of my appointment, there was a strike and all the hospitals were closed. My mother was so worried about the Crohn's threat, she paid to fast track me in a private hospital. At this point I had been off gluten for six months. I had a double scope test and then consultations with a gastroenterologist.

Oh, bollox, I'm a coeliac.

Armed with the notes from the nutritionist and some new kitchen gadgets from my aunty, I started to experiment. But back in college, I was so tired and there were so few food options for me, I decided to eat meat again. I would prep the veg and my friend Tommy would bring the meat. (Insert dirty joke here.) I made fruity quinoa bars to nibble on during lectures. But I was still floundering.

My grocery bills sky-rocketed as I stocked up on gluten-free breads, pastas, sauces, cereals and snacks. I needed a part-time job just to cover food. And I was still getting poisoned in restaurants because I was too embarrassed to explain coeliac disease to the waiters.

Still, things were on the up. I was back to being the bionic bunny. I returned to surfing and I joined the college gym, where I took up weightlifting again. I attended all my early morning lectures and partied at night too. I no longer hurt when I ate. I was alive!

However, I wasn't invincible. Never mind the restaurants, I occasionally poisoned myself – usually with sauces, sometimes with booze. Barley was the most common culprit. I was tired of all my favourite foods being off the menu. This is when I first dreamed of writing a cookbook.

I started making lists of all the things I missed so much – lasagne, chowder, pizza, pasta tuna bake, banana bread, doughnuts, hamburgers, apple crumble. And I thought about the new foods I would never get to try, like the fresh Cornish pasties everyone was raving about in Galway that summer.

I put my scientist's hat on, turned my kitchen into a laboratory and pondered what percentages of fats versus proteins would give the best texture to cakes. Some recipes were an instant hit – check out Coconut Banana Muffins with Molten Dark-Chocolate Core – while others went straight to the recipe graveyard. So long, Hemp Protein Muffins!

I had always been a baker. Now, dish by dish, I became a cook. I grew more and more fascinated with flavours and ingredients. It was no longer simply an exercise in making gluten-free food – it became a search for taste and the optimum fuel to feed my body.

As I became more confident with my recipes, I started guerrilla testing on friends and family. I would show up at their houses with baked treats which I pretended I couldn't eat myself. It wasn't until they'd scoffed the lot and felt sorry for me that I told them the truth.

I began cooking for events at the Gyreum Ecolodge in Sligo, making most of the recipes gluten free, with many dairy free and vegan as well. No one noticed that they were eating 'free from' food. They just made happy noises and asked me later why they didn't have puffy bellies or feel sluggish and sleepy!

At St Angela's, which I graduated from with extra honours in 2016, the chefs who ran the course were amazing forward thinkers and allowed me to adapt every single recipe on the course to a gluten-free version. This way, myself and the rest of the class got to see just how tasty gluten free could be. I may have been the first person in the country to have ever completed a full culinary arts programme entirely gluten free.

I still can't believe my luck, sometimes, that I got my place in St Angela's and was able to fulfil my culinary-studies dream. Life looks very different now than I had pictured it coming out of college and, while there have been a fair few bumps and dips along the way, I wouldn't change a thing. Woolly hats and wet hair are the name of the game now, and my high heels have been hung up as decoration for the time being. While it might seem bonkers to many that I swapped my pursuit of science to food, I must say that my early-onset midlife crisis couldn't have come too soon. Waking up every morning knowing I'm doing what I love, surrounded by good people, with the ocean at my door and mountains at my back is the best feeling in the world! That's all from me for now, folks – get cracking into the recipes and, if you need me, I'll be in the sea!

Ready, Steady, Go

So where do you start?

After I found out I was a coeliac, I simply focused on the food, pining forlornly for baguettes and stumbling around trying to make all my favourite dishes gluten free (though that did largely work out in the end).

If I could go back and mentor 19-year-old me, besides telling her to stop bleaching her hair, I would say take a more well-rounded approach to cooking healthy food, and not to go spending every cent on silly pre-packaged gluten-free (GF) fodder or to obsess over the calories and carbs. Simple healthy food, for me, is all about balance. Yes, I eat homemade food that's ideally sustainably sourced and organic where possible. But I also won't beat myself up if I have a few drinks and a big bag of chipper chips afterwards.

A NOTE ON MEASUREMENTS

As you go on, you'll notice that the recipes are listed in cups, tablespoons and teaspoons as well as grams and mls. It is really important to me that recipes are easy and quick to make – that way you get to spend more time enjoying good food and less time squinting at the numbers on the scales.

So that there's no confusion, I use a set of standard American cups. I have a couple of different sets of these – plastic ones on a ring that are handy and portable and a snazzy china set that were a gift from my best friend. But if I'm being honest, once I got the knack of measuring things out, I didn't worry about it so much. Now I'll use the normal teacups, tablespoons and teaspoons that are in any old kitchen if I don't have my measuring cups to hand. There are just a few recipes where the measurements need to be super, super exact – e.g. the churros recipe on page 69 goes nutso if you don't measure the xanthan gum right!

Having said all that, sometimes, especially with a recipe you've never tried before, it can be reassuring to have the exactness of the scales. I got my little digital one in a run-of-the-mill supermarket for less than €15 and the batteries are cheap to replace. If you're not too familiar with using scales, just look up handy tips online about things like 'zero balancing' to speed you up as you cook and bake. For me, this was a handy skill left over from measuring things in chemistry labs!

I believe taste is a very personal thing. I like flavours to be intense, spicy, salty and sweet. I would recommend that the first time you make any recipe you go with the quantities given, see how you like the flavour and adjust accordingly. For soups and sauces, different quantities of liquid will give you a thicker or thinner consistency, so again adjust as you like.

A NOTE ON INGREDIENTS

As you will see below, I think it's downright daft how much we spend on food these days, especially food that's poor quality. So I won't say anything about good foods or bad foods but, where possible and affordable, I always try to get sustainably caught/farmed seafood and organic meat. I only ever buy free-range eggs, and all the egg-loving recipes in this book have been created with medium-sized organic free-range eggs. (Have you seen the life of a battery hen? The stuff of nightmares.) I try to get organic veggies too, but if I'm feeling thrifty this will apply more to the salad department than things with thick skin – e.g. lemons, avocados, butternut squash and so on.

RESOURCES

YouTube

Funny one, I know, but it's how I found Lean Secrets and Tone It Up. While both these sites are more for fitness and fat loss, they were also the first places I saw non-coeliacs choosing to go GF for health reasons. Having a bubbly person chat you through tasty recipes is a lot more fun than reading lists of things you can't eat. Go explore. There are literally thousands of YouTubers talking about all kinds of delicious food.

Friends and family

My family were a huge support during that rough year of diagnosis and my friends have been diligent in taste-testing dishes so that the recipes are not just 'oh, that's not bad for gluten-free stuff' but instead are 'holy crap, can I stuff all this in my face?' scrumptious. Your best chance of speedy,

successful implementation of a gluten-free diet is getting others to help. I'm not saying they all need to go GF, but getting to eat the same meal as the other people in your house can make it feel a bit more comfortable and normal when you're starting out. I'm now sending my girls home with jars of Costa del Granola (page 39) after surf trips and muffins (page 50) for the car journey!

Health food stores

Long associated in my brain with hippies and incense, this was where I went in the early days to escape the sawdust pharmacy bread. I now buy my staples in the supermarket (more on that below) because they're half the price. However, for good-quality healthy fats (virgin coconut oil and fish-oil supplements) and tasty GF flavour boosts (Worcestershire sauce or miso paste), this is the place to go. For lazy days, it can also be good to stock up on things like high-quality tinned soups or fresh GF ravioli.

Asian markets

I've Susan Jane White to thank for this inspiration. I've long been the eejit spending a ton on things like spices, goji berries, gluten-free noodles and rose water (yeah, that one's for skincare but whatever) in supermarkets and health shops. These things can be literally half the price in the delicious-smelling Asian markets, where potentially boring things like grocery shopping are made far more exciting; it's also a great way to expand your taste horizons.

Aldi

Yep, you read that right. Seems strange to tout a big, bad supermarket, right? Wrong. Aldi is basically my best mate

who's like, 'Here, Finn, I hear you're a bit strapped for cash
but want tasty food to eat. I'll sort you out!' These lads are
at the forefront of decent gluten-free sections and their
free-from range also tends to be organic. Tick and tick.
Now, after many years, I've pretty much gotten to the
food-snob place where I only eat healthy homemade treats,
but feck that if you're just getting into the swing of things.
These guys do great biscuits (the ginger ones are my fave),
an Irish soda bread that is possibly the closest thing to 'real'
bread I've tasted from a shop in a long time and, finally, the
pancakes. While terribly bold, they taste just like the ones
my nana used to give me when I was little. Extra brownie
points for recreating happy childhood memories! Finally,
their GF oats are the cheapest ones I've found so far that
actually come in a decent quantity. For the more savvy
shopper, this is also where I pick up my pantry essentials like
chia seeds, milled linseeds, ground almonds and maple syrup,
which you will later see are fairly crucial!

YOUR KITCHEN

Yep, you guessed it! A bit of clever prepping will set you
flying and with this book you'll be whipping things up faster
than Gordon Ramsey can say f***.

There are some important things to think about if you're
coeliac or wheat intolerant and non-gluten-free folk are using
the same kitchen. Cross-contamination is a bitch; it's the
source of most poisonings. To be safe:

· Keep GF carbs, breads, pastas, crackers, etc. away from
  the wheaty ones.
· Use plastic chopping boards instead of wooden ones –
  sneaky flour stays in the cracks.
· Keep a GF butter dish separate from the main one.
· If you're a toast fiend, get your own toaster or use the grill.
· Don't prepare extremely wheat-floury recipes for other
  people. It took me five years to not be this thick. I love
  to bake and every year I make gingerbread houses and
  themed cakes (think *The Lion, the Witch and the Wardrobe*
  and *Frozen* Elsa-doll cakes) for my cousin's kids. Last
  Christmas I managed to inhale a ton of flour (which
  subsequently went into my tummy) while making the Elsa
  cake and knocked myself out of the festival humour for a
  solid two days. If you simply must make non-GF stuff –
  you work in a restaurant baking/are too skint to bake for
  others with GF flour – then a) get someone else to do the
  measuring, sifting and stirring in of the flour or b) wear a
  surgical-type mask. It'll look a little odd (for comic effect,
  draw an eyeball on it) but at least your insides won't get
  damaged and you won't feel like shit!

ARMOURY

If prior to this you thought preparing a meal was taking food out of a takeaway container and putting it on a plate, you will be pleased to know that the recipes in this book are extremely straightforward. No soufflés and nothing so complicated that it requires you to sweat excessively with worry. You will need some basics, but they're inexpensive enough:

- Plastic chopping boards
- Big and small sharp knives
- Large mixing bowl
- Medium-sized mixing bowl
- Hand blender – otherwise known as a stick or immersion blender (and most likely referred to hereafter as the ssssghhh machine, since that's the noise it makes)
- Rectangular casserole dish, Pyrex or ceramic (33cm x 23 cm), which can be used for pasta bakes, roasts or tray bakes like brownies
- Bread tin (1 lb) – standard smaller size
- Springform baking tin (23cm or 25cm) – don't look at me like that: it's not fancy. I got mine in Lidl and it's brilliant. I also use the bottom bit by itself for roasting sweet potatoes
- Round pie dish (23cm) – also useful for baking chicken breasts
- Muffin tray – because who doesn't like muffins?
- Decent non-stick frying pan – too many pancakes are lost every day to crap frying pans
- Proper measuring-cup set – I have nice ones a friend from America gave me, but ordinary ones can be easily sourced from the €2 shop (classy, I know, but much more accurate than bog standard teacups, tablespoons and teaspoons)

Fancy extras:
Waffle iron or toasty maker (don't share these with non-GF users); silicon ice-cube trays (can also be used as chocolate moulds for cool shapes).

Useful consumables:
Baking parchment; tin foil; leftover glass jars from sauces (good for storing dry goods or as a hipster drinking glass and lunch-transportation device); string (for tying up things wrapped in baking parchment). I'm a bit anti cling film and plastic bags – bad for the enviro and the fishies and all that.

The Most
Meal of

Important
the Day

Also known as breakfast, or the time when you get to eat stuff smothered in syrup and no one bats an eyelid …

Breakfast can be a bit of a minefield for eating gluten free. Things that should be safe in theory, well, aren't. The main culprits are rice- and corn-based cereals that are actually sweetened with barley malt or oats. Oats are naturally GF but they are generally grown in the same fields and processed in the same factories as wheat, making them a no-go. Then there are all the breads, croissants, Danishes and other pastry delights (apple lattices were my downfall) that are off the menu.

So what's left, you ask? Plenty! The wonderful twist is that many of those old favourites are also the source of the dreaded energy crash that usually hits around 11 a.m. The recipes here should have you hopping out of bed and looking forward to breakfast, not skipping it. Since no two days are the same, the breakfasts are split up into my everyday staples, the muscle makers (for days off and after heavy training sessions) and the less saintly ones (for weekend treats and special occasions).

A personal favourite is the churros on page 69, which I like to serve with strong coffee, a good read and some of my very broken Spanish.

Everyday Staples

These recipes are my go-to, eat-every-day old faithfuls.
Lots of them, like the granolas on pages 39, 42 and 44
can be made in advance so you get to spend more time
in the morning relaxing into your day instead of in a
panicked whirlwind of cooking everything from scratch.

Ready, Steady Regression Porridge

This Ready Brek-like porridge is made with millet flakes, which produce a soft, easy-on-the-tum mix. It brings back happy childhood memories of when the only way to coax you out of bed mid-December was the promise of raspberry jam in your porridge!

For maximum laziness, you can divide the millet flakes, water and salt evenly between two bowls and blast 'em in the microwave for 1¹/₂ to 2 minutes each. Alternatively you can make them with a little more love in a pot on a medium heat, stirring regularly. Millet flakes aren't like oat flakes so it's best to cook them for a long time to avoid a dry texture in the middle of the flake. Don't soak them, as they go weird and soggy. Yakky!

TO SERVE
Pop the millet porridge in a bowl with your favourite milk, a big dollop of jam and an episode of *Power Rangers* on TV.

SERVES 2 PEOPLE PRETENDING THEY AREN'T ADULTS

1 cup (100g) millet flakes

2 cups (470ml) water

pinch of salt

milk of your choice *I like goat's milk with this, but it's a little strong for some folks*

dollop of your favourite jam to swirl through the porridge

Oat Yeah, Baby

I'm a huge fan of porridge in the winter months. It's sweet, warm and sets you up nicely for a day of battling the elements. (Galway City on a blustery November morning takes the make-up clean off your face.)

Warning: oats are not suitable for all coeliacs, as they contain a protein which about 1 per cent of coeliacs can't tolerate. I reintroduced oats into my diet slowly, having chatted with the doc first. I recommend you do the same and see how your body feels!

SERVES 2 GRUMPY MORNING HUMANS

1 banana

1 cup (100g) GF porridge of choice

handful raisins, soaked overnight in cold tea or water with a dash of vanilla extract

2 cups (470ml) water

¼ tsp cinnamon

honey, maple syrup or sugar-free syrup *I like Walden Farm's Pancake Syrup, which lives in the sports nutrition shop*

milk of your choice

toasted nuts and seeds of your choice

1   Peel and chop the banana. A slightly green banana means less of a sugar bomb on your system, releasing sugars slowly over the morning. I found this great for getting me through early morning lectures in college.

2   Put the oats, chopped banana, soaked raisins and 2 cups of water in a pot over a medium heat. Add the cinnamon as the water starts to bubble. Stir continuously. The more you stir, the smoother the texture. If you're lucky enough in your worldly travels to come across a spurtle – a Scottish wooden device engineered solely for the sake of smooth porridge – use it! If you don't have one but are a true porridge fancier, some online research could be in order.

3   The porridge should be smooth, hot and a little chewy when done. Remove to a bowl and add milk and sweetener of choice. My favourite combination is almond milk and maple syrup.

A great trick I've picked up from my mom is to have a jar of toasted seeds on hand. This is such a nice addition and saves you having to dry fry something in the morning and risk setting the house on fire. Simply heat a dry pan to medium-high and bung in a mix of your favourite seeds.

I tend to do sunflower and pumpkin seeds together. Sesame seeds are great too but should be done in the pan on their own, as they toast much faster due to their itty-bitty size. Once the seeds have cooled they can be stored in an airtight glass container for weeks.

Danish Breakfast Brød

One summer a fantastic opportunity brought me to Denmark to speak at a geological conference on ancient corals. My group travelled outside Copenhagen to a little area called Faxe, renowned among fossil hunters. Our guesthouse mama provided us with a massive breakfast. We were plonked in front of a table laden with homemade yogurt, fresh fruit and eggs from her very own chickens. But she hadn't been warned there was a coeliac in the gang. She grumbled about the organisers making her look bad, then her eyes lit up and she legged it into the kitchen.

What she brought back was a game changer. An amazing, crunchy, nutty, moreish sort of bread. I'd never seen anything like it. Even small and thinly sliced, it's so rich you can't eat too much (challenge accepted, says you) but, oh my god, it was fabulous! All I knew was that nuts and seeds were being held together by eggs. Returning home, I played around with different combinations until I created the winning loaf.

MAKES A 1 LB LOAF – 12–16 SLICES

Dry Bowl

1 ½ cups (150g) GF oats

1 cup (140g) sunflower seeds

½ cup (55g) ground or whole linseeds

½ cup (70g) other nuts or seeds, e.g. almonds or pumpkin seeds

1 tsp salt – I like pink Himalayan

Wet Bowl

4 tbsp milled chia seeds

2 cups (470ml) water

1 egg

2 tbsp olive or sunflower oil

1 tbsp maple syrup or honey

1　Preheat the oven to 180°C.
2　In the wet bowl, mix the water with the milled chia seeds and stir after a few minutes. The chia seeds will magically take on an eggy consistency.
3　Bung all the dry-bowl ingredients together and stir with a wooden spoon.
4　Give the wet bowl another stir to stop the chia seeds from clumping together and add the egg, oil and maple syrup or honey. This mix will look a bit like frog spawn but fear not, dear reader, you won't regret it.
5　Add the wet-bowl mixture to the dry bowl and mix until you have a wet dough. Allow this to relax in the bowl for about half an hour. Be patient! You're giving the oats time to soak up the water for a lovely bready consistency. (Sometimes the dough relaxes so much that it soaks up all the water and gets a bit dry. If this happens, add another $^1/_2$ cup (120ml) of water and stir again.
6　Now line your bread tin with baking parchment and pour in the mix. Smooth the top of the dough with the flat side of the wooden spoon to give the finished loaf a nicer appearance.
7　Bake for 45–55 minutes. Baking will always take less time with a fan-assisted oven. As my oven likes to act up sometimes, the loaf can take up to an hour to bake. You know your bread's done if it makes a hollow sound when you knock on it. Yes, knock. Like on a door. Hullo, brød, are you ready? Ja!
8　Take it out and let it cool. I can be bold and sneak chunks off things before they cool, but do not compromise the structural integrity, people. This brød will crumble if you mess with it when it's hot!

TO SERVE

It's a very versatile little loaf. You can pre-slice the whole thing and store it in the freezer, taking out slices as you need them. It's even tastier when toasted and goes well with the Fry Not? (page 72) or Poached Eggs on Toast with Green Things (page 36). For leisurely lunches, serve alongside one of the soups in the next section.

TASTY TIP

For vegans, swap the egg with an extra tablespoon of chia seeds mixed with $\frac{1}{2}$ cup (120ml) of water. It will have a slightly more crumbly texture so do make sure to let it cool completely before slicing!

Poached Eggs on Toast with Green Things

A simple breakfast with a few greens starts you off perfectly for the day. Use asparagus if you're feeling posh, but steamed spinach is my favourite.

SERVES 2 HUMANS IN NEED OF A BIT OF GREENERY

4 slices Danish Brød (page 34)

2 large handfuls baby leaf spinach or 1 handful asparagus spears

2–4 eggs *I'm a protein fan so I like 2 eggs for myself*

butter for the toast *or olive oil if you're dairy free*

salt and pepper to taste

squeeze of lemon for the greens

1 Lash your bread in the toaster.

2 Trim your greens. When it's asparagus, I trim the ends off diagonally and then cut the remaining stalks in two. I use a bamboo steamer over the pot that's poaching the egg. If you don't have one you can improvise with a metal colander and the pot's lid!

3 If it seems condescending to tell you how to cook an egg, know that we spent an entire day learning to cook eggs properly (boiling, poaching, frying etc.) on my culinary course.

4 Pour water into a small pot to a depth of 4–5cm and bring to a simmer – boiling is a bit too boisterous for these guys. While the water is heating up, you can put your steamer over it to ensure the asparagus is fully cooked when your eggs are done; if you're using spinach you don't need to put it in until later.

5   For the eggs, use the freshest you can find. This means the white of the egg is still firm and not watery and has a better chance of holding together! I'm a total wuss when it comes to poaching eggs so I crack them one at a time – oh so gently – into a little jug. Then, when the water is simmering, I swirl it around with a fork (because my chef teacher told me to) and carefully slide the eggs in. I like to leave my eggs in till the yolk is fairly firm – that's up to 5 minutes.
But you can decide for yourself – less for runny, more for solid. Once the eggs are in, lash the steamer back on top of the pot and turn the heat down a bit, as the steamer keeps the heat in.

TO SERVE

I butter the toast, pop on the spinach with a squeeze of lemon, slide the eggs on top and season with salt and pepper. It's like a healthy Eggs Florentine. With asparagus, I serve them on the side with a drizzle of lemon, a knob of butter and a twist of black pepper.

Costa del Granola

A veggie restaurant I used to work in made granola fresh every week and served it with organic yogurt and fresh fruit. The morning staff all enjoyed a hearty bowl of it. I like this recipe so much I often eat it as a sweet snack when watching a movie or as a dessert.

1　Preheat the oven to 160°C.

2　In a small jug, mix the sunflower oil or coconut oil with the honey or maple syrup.

3　In a big bowl, mix the oats, dried fruit, seeds and cinnamon together. Don't put the desiccated coconut in at this point as it can burn!

4　Pour the oil and honey mix into the big bowl and incorporate until everything is thoroughly coated. I recommend using a wooden spoon, not your hands. Cover a baking tray with baking parchment and spoon the granola mix onto the surface. Spread evenly.

5　Bake for up to 30 minutes, mixing every 10 minutes to ensure even browning. The longer you cook it, the crunchier it will be. Some people like it super crunchy but I prefer the chewiness of the oats when taken out at around 15–20 minutes.

6　Remove from the oven at the desired time, lash in the toasted desiccated coconut and allow to cool.

MAKES ONE 2L JAR

½ cup (120ml) sunflower or coconut oil, melted

½ cup (170g) runny honey
or ¹/₂ cup (120ml) maple syrup for a vegan option

3 cups (300g) GF oats

½ cup (80g) dried diced papaya

½ cup (80g) dried diced pineapple

3 tbsp linseeds

½ cup (70g) sunflower seeds

1 tsp cinnamon

½ cup (40g) desiccated coconut, toasted in a dry pan till lightly golden

TO SERVE

To maintain the tropical vibe, I like to serve this with slightly exotic fruits. Not an apple in sight! Go with things like mangos, when they're cheaper in season, kiwis and bananas. Top it off with a nice natural or coconut yogurt.

If you've got a sweet tooth like me and suffer from dessert guilt, this can be served with Greek yogurt and a splash of maple syrup for a healthier treat.

TASTY TIPS

For a clumpier granola, add a bit more honey. With a little less honey, the granola will be very fine and can be used as an oaty cereal and served with fresh chilled milk.

Buckwheat Date Chocolate Heaven ... er, sorry ... Granola

I am a complete granola snob or, probably more accurately, a grump. When I pick up a pack of granola in the shop – especially the fancy-looking ones – I'm downright miffed. It's basically a tiny box of some grains mixed with a shed-load of sugar and a few sad-looking raisins. Not so with this delicious chocolatey version. Good friends who've gone home with bags of it call it 'Finn's healthy Coco Pops'!

MAKES ONE 2 LITRE JAR

½ cup (120ml) coconut oil, melted, or sunflower oil

½ cup (120ml) date syrup

3 cups (500g) toasted buckwheat

1 cup (100g) GF oats *leave out if you can't have oats and add an extra cup of buckwheat instead*

1 cup (140g) sunflower seeds

½ cup (70g) hazelnuts

3 tbsp cocoa powder *or 2 tbsp of cacao for super healthiness*

½ cup (80g) raisins

1   Preheat your oven to 160°C.

2   Mix the coconut oil and date syrup in a small jug. Lash all the dry ingredients into a bowl except the raisins, as they go all weird and burnt in the oven. Pour the oil and syrup over the dry mix. Line a baking tray with baking parchment and spread the granola mix out evenly on it.

3   Bake for up to 25 minutes, mixing every 10 minutes to ensure even browning. The longer you cook it, the crunchier it will be. Some people like it extra crunchy, but I prefer the chewiness when taken out after around 15–20 minutes. Add the raisins, stir through and allow to cool before storing.

TO SERVE

Serve with milk for healthy Coco Pops, serve with stewed fruit and Greek yogurt for a hearty winter breakfast or add ¼ cup (60ml) more date syrup and press into the baking tray to make granola bars that can be cut into squares. For the granola bars, cut the shapes as soon as the mix comes out of the oven so the granola doesn't just crack.

Mother Hubbard's Bare Cupboard Granola

This one came about when I went to make breakfast for some guests and found that my cupboards were more bare than buff ...

MAKES ONE 2 LITRE JAR

½ cup (120ml) sunflower oil

⅓ cup (110g) honey

3 cups (300g) GF oats

1 cup (160g) raisins

2 tsp cinnamon

1 cup (140g) almonds, chopped

1. Preheat your oven to 160°C.
2. Mix the sunflower oil and honey in a small jug. Bung all the dry ingredients in a bowl except the raisins, as they burn quickly in the oven. Pour the oil and honey over the dry ingredients and mix well. Line a baking tray with baking parchment and spread the mixture out evenly on it.
3. Bake for up to 25 minutes, mixing every 10 minutes to ensure even browning. The longer you cook it the crunchier it will be. Some people like it super crunchy, but I prefer the chewiness when taken out at around 15–20 minutes. Add the raisins, mix well and cool.

TO SERVE

Delish by the handful. Also perfect over stewed fruit and Greek yogurt or with milk as a cereal.

The Three in One

This is a super-simple breakfast of stewed apples, Greek yogurt and toasted seeds that's handy if you're legging it out the door to college, work or wherever. All the components are prepared the night before. I make a big jar of the compote on a Sunday to keep me going all week.

1   Roughly chop your apples. I like to leave the skin on for the extra fibre and less effort. Lash the chopped apple into a pot with some cinnamon, the raisins and the maple syrup.

2   Stew away over a low heat until the apples are nice and soft. Transfer to a container and allow the compote to cool before storing it in the fridge.

3   Toast the seeds and almonds in a dry pan on a medium heat. Shake them around a bit so they toast evenly. You might as well do loads and keep them in a jar for other days.

4   Spoon the compote into a bowl, top with Greek yogurt and shimmy the seeds over the top. For vegan folk, coconut yogurt is an absolutely ingenious alternative. If you need a little more sweetness in your life, drizzle with maple syrup.

SERVES AS MANY AS YOU LIKE

Apple Compote ~
makes roughly one 1l jar

8 large cooking apples, coarsely chopped

pinch of cinnamon

½ cup (80g) of California raisins

2 tbsp maple syrup *you can leave this out if you use eating apples instead of cooking ones*

Toppings

½ cup (70g) pumpkin seeds

½ cup (70g) sunflower seeds

½ cup (70g) flaked almonds

Greek yogurt

The Three in One, page 45

Moroccan Surfer's Breakfast

When my godfather came back from Morocco a few years ago, he made me this amazing breakfast of spiced couscous, fruit and yogurt. I loved it so much I ate it every morning after rowing training. Fast forward to the time when I realised that couscous is a wheat derivative. Damn! So here's the recipe revamped and reloaded with a higher protein content. The simple solution? Swap the couscous for quinoa. At 15 per cent protein, this grain gives serious bang for its buck.

SERVES 2 HUNGRY HUMANS

1 cup (170g) uncooked quinoa

2 cups (470g) water

optional spices: 1 cinnamon stick or ½ tsp ground cinnamon, 1 star anise or a few cloves

selection of fruit, chopped *e.g. apple, banana, mango, nectarine*

yogurt *I'm a devotee of Greek-style yogurt*

1 Rinse the quinoa in a sieve under cold water for a few minutes. This gets rid of the coating that can make it taste bitter. Some folks toast the quinoa before cooking but, frankly, I never bother. Put the quinoa, water and spices in a small pot and bring to a simmer. Cook for 10 minutes with a lid until the quinoa absorbs all the water.

2 For extra fluffiness turn the heat off and leave it for 3 more minutes in the pot. The steam does the last bit of work. Then remove the cinnamon stick, star anise or cloves if you have used them.

3 Scoop the quinoa into bowls, top with your choice of chopped fruit and yogurt. I like to add a little cinnamon and maple syrup as well.

Broke-Student Breakfast Muffins

Muffins were the first thing I ever learned to make when I was little. Fairy cakes were never the done thing in my house – too small and too boring. So I used to help Mum make muffins and then do a mini Darina Allen cookery show with play dough for anyone who was over. I even had her haircut! This recipe is based on the one that's at home in the family cookbook, where all the pages stick together. My variation is GF with a few bits added. I like to make a batch of these the Sunday before a busy week so I can grab one (but really it's two) on my way out the door in the mornings.

MAKES 12

2 cups (240g) Doves Farm GF self-raising flour (brown or white)

1 cup (60g) ground almonds

pinch of salt

1 tsp GF baking powder

1 tsp ground cinnamon

¾ cup (70g) chopped nuts or seeds e.g. walnuts, sunflower or pumpkin seeds

¾ cup (180ml) sunflower oil

2 eggs

⅓ cup (80ml) maple syrup

1 large or 2 small mashed bananas

½ cup (60g) grated apple or carrot (optional)

1   Preheat the oven to 180°C.

2   The easiest way to make these is to have a dry bowl and a wet bowl and then lash the wet into the dry.

3   Dry bowl: sift the flour, then add the ground almonds, salt, baking powder, cinnamon and your chosen nuts or seeds.

4   Wet bowl: pour in the oil, crack in the eggs and whisk. When nicely mixed, add the maple syrup and mix again. Now add the mashed banana and grated apple or carrot, if using, and – you've guessed it! – mix it all up.

5   Add the dry mix to the wet. Stir until you have a thick batter.

6   Lightly grease a muffin tin with a little oil. I rarely use muffin cases, as I don't see the point in constantly trying to avoid eating paper. Spoon the batter into the muffin tin.

7   Pop 'em in the oven. They should take 14–20 minutes, depending on your oven. Use the butt of a teaspoon to check if they're done. If you stick it in the middle and pull it out again, there should be no residue on the spoon. If there is residue, pop the muffins back in the oven for another 5 minutes.

TO SERVE

Eat them on the run or chillin' with a glass of milk or cup of tea. These guys keep for up to four days in an airtight container. If they're a little old and going a bit hard, they can be 'refreshed' by popping them in the microwave for 20–30 seconds.

Muscle-Maker Breakfasts

Protein is a vital macro-nutrient for muscle repair.
While I was working with a personal trainer I learned
a lot about how a hearty protein-rich breakfast not only
sets you up to feel fuller longer, but is also integral
to repairing muscle that has been broken down after
strenuous exercise.

Baywatch Breakfast Proats

Proats is the jock name for a breakfast of protein and oats. They are an easy way to up your protein intake for the day, are more fun than a protein shake and keep you fuller for longer than a bowl of porridge. This is my go-to proats mix for the summer – kind of like The Hoff and a pina colada mixed together.

1   Pop the oats and water in a bowl and into the microwave. In a high-powered microwave they'll only need 1–2 minutes. If it's super-hot when you take it out, add a bit of cold water. Never stir protein powder into something that is super hot, as it will curdle and go all gross!

2   Stir in the protein powder and then bung the rest of the ingredients on top!

TOP TIP

Since protein-powder mixes tend to already be sweetened you don't need to add any syrups, etc. on top. This is great for reducing your overall sugar consumption in a day, as I find breakfast is usually the meal where this can be my downfall.

SERVES 1 BUFF HUMAN IN THE MORNING

½ cup (50g) GF oats *high in soluble and insoluble fibre, good source of slow-release carbs*

1 cup (235ml) water *instead of milk, fewer calories overall*

1 scoop (30g) GF vanilla protein of your choice *generally I use Kinetica, Optimum Nutrition or Platinum and Diamond Nutrition, but you could use a vegan one if you're having a problem with dairy*

1 tbsp toasted desiccated coconut *healthy fats, fibre and tastiness*

2 pineapple rings (in juice, not syrup) *natural sweetness, good source of vitamin C*

1 tbsp milled seed mix *crunchy nuttiness, source of healthy fats and fibre*

Malibu Muscle Barbie Proats

Super simple, but with the addition of some frozen mixed forest fruits, delicious purple porridge will ensue! This pink powerhouse is super simple and will keep you fuelled up for a busy day or can be had as a sweet treat after the gym

SERVES 1 BUFF HUMAN IN THE MORNING

½ cup (50g) GF oats *high in soluble and insoluble fibre, good source of slow-release carbs*

1 cup (235ml) water *instead of milk, fewer calories overall*

½ cup (50g) frozen mixed forest fruits

1 scoop (30g) GF vanilla protein of your choice *generally I use Kinetica, Optimum Nutrition or Platinum and Diamond Nutrition, but you could use a vegan one if you're having a problem with dairy*

1 tbsp toasted desiccated coconut *healthy fats, fibre and tastiness*

1 tbsp milled seed mix *crunchy nuttiness, source of healthy fats and fibre*

1 Pop the oats, water and frozen fruit in a bowl and into the microwave. In a high-powered microwave they'll only need 1–2 minutes. If it's super-hot when you take it out, add a bit of cold water. Never stir protein powder into something that is really hot, as it will curdle.

2 Stir in the protein powder and then pop the coconut and seeds on top and you're done.

Reese's Cup Proats

While this is technically breakfast, I usually eat it before bed on days when I've been training particularly hard. It's kind of like a Reese's Cup and proats had an amazing baby!

Divide the oats and the water between two bowls. Slice the banana and put half on top of each bowl. The banana gets a lovely caramel consistency while it cooks. Pop each bowl in the microwave – if it's high-powered you'll only need 1–2 minutes. (You can also make them on the hob in a small pot – it just takes a little longer.) When you take it out, if it's really hot add a bit of cold water. Never stir protein powder into something that is super-hot as it will curdle. Stir in the protein powder, cocoa or cacao powder and peanut butter.

TO SERVE
This gets a great crunch if topped with a sprinkle of cacao nibs or mixed seeds if you have them.

SERVES 2 FOR BREAKFAST OR AFTER THE GYM

1 cup (100g) GF oats

2 cups (470ml) water

1 banana

2 scoops (60g) vanilla or chocolate protein powder

2 tsp cocoa or cacao powder

2 tbsp peanut butter

Popeye Protein Pancakes

I've always been a complete pancake fiend. These ones are also full of healthy carbs and fats. They are the perfect treat with bacon and maple syrup or good as gold with Walden Farm Pancake Syrup and 0% fat Greek yogurt. These guys have become a bit of a Sunday ritual for me and I hope they will for you too. Also they're even better than a hug if you're having a crappy day.

MAKES 1 BIG STACK OF FAT
PANCAKES OR ENOUGH FOR
2 WHEN SERVED WITH OTHER
BITS

1 cup (100g) GF oats

½ tsp GF baking powder

2 eggs

1 standard scoop (30g) vanilla protein powder

1 tsp cinnamon

2 cups (470ml) water

1   Simplicity is key here. Lash all the ingredients in a big jug and blend till smooth with a hand blender.

2   Heat up your most pancake-friendly pan (one of those non-stick fellows), put it on a medium to high heat and drop in a dollop of coconut oil – a tablespoon-ish. This is usually enough for me to cook the whole batch – I just give the pan a wipe with some kitchen towel to get rid of any excess so the pancakes don't feel like they've been deep-fried. Depending on your level of pancake-chef confidence, you can either make a tester pancake to see if the pan's hot enough or you can just jump right in. Use roughly 3 tbsps of batter per pancake.

3   Once the pan is hot enough it should take about 30 seconds on each side for the pancakes to cook. When the first side has bubbles, flip it over and count it out. If the pancakes look too dark, just reduce the heat a bit. You will get anywhere up to 10 smaller pancakes, and I like to put my grill on low and pile them up on a plate to keep them warm while I cook up the rest of the batch.

TO SERVE

My favourite way to serve these is with some crispy bacon on the side, smothered with Walden Farm Pancake Syrup and a big pot of fresh brewed coffee (you could try the Beef-cake Coffee on page 316 for a ruined breakfast) to wash it all down.

I also stack the pancakes with Greek yoghurt and stewed berries. To stew the berries, simply heat frozen mixed forest fruits or raspberries in a pot on the stove or in a bowl in the microwave until they are steaming and cooked through.

Protein Power Yogurt

This is so simple it almost seems silly writing about it, but it's such a handy protein-packing breakfast that's perfect for taking in the morning on the way to college or work.

SERVES 1 AMBITIOUS MORNING HUMAN

200g 0% fat Greek yogurt *e.g. Fage Total or Glenisk*

1 scoop (30g) your choice of whey protein *my favourite for this is Kinetica vanilla*

1 tbsp desiccated coconut

handful toasted seeds – sunflower, pumpkin etc.

handful blueberries

handful raspberries

1 In a bowl, or a Tupperware container, stir the scoop of protein into the yogurt until it's all mixed in and there are no lumps of powder.

2 Place a small non-stick pan on the stove over a medium to high heat. I usually just wave my hand over the pan to get an idea if it's warm or not yet.

3 Pop in the coconut first and shimmy it around till it's a light golden-brown colour – this gives it a way nicer flavour then just having it plain. When the coconut is done pour it over the yogurt mix and repeat the same thing with the seeds. You can't toast them all together as the coconut toasts faster than the seeds so it would burn and be yucky!

TO SERVE
Sprinkle with a little cinnamon and honey if you need a little sweetness.

Chocolate Almond Breakfast Mug Cake

This is a handy thing to whip up for a quick breakfast. I've also made it for guests on a diet if they don't want to feel left out of dessert after dinner.

1. Grease the mug with coconut oil – this way, your cake can slide out easily when it's done.
2. In the mug, combine the protein powder, ground almonds, baking powder and cocoa powder.
3. On a plate, mash up the banana. Pop this and the egg white into the mug and stir till it's all combined.
4. Put the mug in the microwave (gasp of horror – a cake in the microwave!) and cook on high for $1^1/_2$–$2^1/_2$ minutes (depending on the power of your microwave). The cake will rise up over the edges of the mug like a horror movie monster. If it's scaring you and you fear that you will lose half of your mug cake, just open the door for a second and it will go back down!
5. When cooked, turn it out onto a plate.

TO SERVE
You can top with Greek yogurt, chopped walnuts and a little maple syrup.

SERVES 1 SAINTLY HUMAN

coconut oil, for greasing

1 scoop (30g) protein powder

½ cup (60g) ground almonds

½ tsp GF baking powder

1 tsp cocoa powder

½ mashed banana – or 1 small one

1 egg white

Slightly Less Saintly Breakfasts

In my house, this is the recipe arsenal taken out and dusted off in the event of a break-up, a celebration (yahoo – a job offer, etc.) or a special occasion (birthday, Christmas and so on). These recipes are decadent till the end, but you will not find one iota of guilt or shame in the ingredients, so enjoy every last bite!

The Trudeau

Sweet and hot, like Canada's prime minister. The first time I had banana pancakes with bacon and maple syrup, I was eight years old, having breakfast with my mom in downtown Toronto. They were so amazing and created such a strong memory that I still know what my mom had – eggs Benedict – and what the mural on the wall was – a big tree and flowering garden.

SERVES 2 LAZY SUNDAY HUMANS

Dry Mix

2 cups (240g) GF self-raising flour
I like Dove's Farm Organic

1 ½ tsp GF baking powder

1 tsp ground cinnamon

pinch of salt – one twist of a salt grinder

Wet Mix

1 cup (240ml) milk

1 cup (240ml) water

2 eggs

2 ripe bananas *i.e. brown-looking skin*

coconut oil or butter for frying

1   Pop all the dry ingredients in a big bowl and mix. If you're feeling fancy you can sift them first.

2   In a big jug, lash in the milk and water, crack in the eggs and chuck in the bananas. Blend with a hand blender.

3   Make a well in the dry mix, pour in the wet mix in and blend. You should have a runny batter. I don't add anything sweet, as there are natural sugars in the banana and I'll probably drown the pancakes in maple syrup later. Pour the batter into a jug.

4   Heat up a good non-stick pan to a medium-high heat. Pancakes can stick to an old crappy pan; this can make you frustrated and lead to your throwing the pan out the window into the back garden – not that I'm admitting I did that, just saying it can happen …

5   To coat the pan, I melt about a tablespoon of oil or butter in it and swirl it around. Then I gently rub the pan down with a piece of kitchen paper, which I'm sure would draw a gasp of horror from most chefs. This blots the excess butter so your pancakes don't feel like they were cooked in grease.

6   I do a tester pancake to make sure the pan is hot enough. It should take 30–50 seconds for bubbles to form on the top of the pancake. Now flip it over and cook for another 30–50 seconds.

7   These pancakes will expand so make them small, i.e. about 2 tablespoons of batter each. If you were around in the nineties, these pancakes should look like the ones Sabrina the Teenage Witch kept dreaming about when she had a pancake addiction. You should be able to get about three at a time in a decent-sized pan.

TO SERVE

I usually serve these pancakes as a stack with a little knob of butter on top, a pile of crispy bacon on the side and drowned in maple syrup. Sorry. I think I just drooled on the laptop.

The Classic Frenchie

The GF crêpe is *magnifique*! If you get a good GF flour it can be even better than a regular crêpe, as GF flours are made of lighter, sweeter ingredients such as rice or tapioca flour.

SERVES 2 RAVENOUS PEOPLE
OR 3 AS A LIGHTER TREAT

½ cup (120ml) water

½ cup (120ml) milk

1 cup (120g) GF plain flour

1 egg *I've tried it with 2 and the pancakes go rubbery*

3 tbsp butter

1   In a jug, mix your water and milk. Sift or chuck your flour into a big bowl. Make a well in the centre, crack in the egg and pour in the water and milk mix. Stir it all up till you have a smooth, runny batter with no floury lumps (yuk) and pop it back in the jug for easy pouring.

2   Put a non-stick pan on a medium to high heat. When the pan is hot, chuck in the butter. When it has melted you can swoosh it around to coat the pan and then pour the excess into the crêpe batter (oooh, decadent, you say). Give the batter a stir to mix in the butter.

3   I always make a mini tester crêpe in case the pan is messing with me and only pretending to be at the right temperature. When the pan is hot enough – i.e. the tester pancake cooks on both sides in about 30 seconds and doesn't stick to the pan – you're ready to go! Use about 3 tablespoons of batter per crêpe and cook one at a time for roughly 30 seconds on each side.

4   Place the cooked crêpes on a plate in a low oven to keep them warm while you finish cooking the rest.

TO SERVE

A plate of lemon wedges and a bowl of sugar look nice on the table. The crêpes are also delish with a few other classic combos such as banana slices and Nutella, peanut butter and raspberry jam, stewed berries and honey, Greek yogurt and flaked almonds and honey.

The Gallant Galette with Gruyère and Crispy Ham

I first tried this classic French savoury pancake in a lovely little café in Ennistymon in the wild west of Ireland. The galette is naturally gluten free, as it's made with buckwheat. But sometimes it can be hard to find buckwheat flour that's certified gluten free. If you're a coeliac or have to be strictly GF, blitz toasted buckwheat groats thoroughly and sift them to get a safer flour!

SERVES 2

1 cup (235ml) water
1 cup (235ml) buttermilk
1 cup (120g) buckwheat flour
2 eggs
2 tbsp butter

For the Filling
⅓ cup (75g) grated Gruyère cheese
½ cup (80g) sliced ham
¼ cup (35g) chopped walnuts

1 In a jug, mix your water and buttermilk. Sift or chuck your flour into a big bowl. Make a well in the centre, crack in the eggs and pour in the water and buttermilk mix. Stir it all up till you have a smooth, runny batter with no floury lumps.

2 Put a non-stick pan on a medium to high heat. When the pan is hot, chuck in the butter. When it has melted, swoosh it around to coat the pan and then pour the excess into the galette batter. Give it a stir to mix in the butter.

3 When the pan is hot – i.e. a test galette cooked on both sides in about 30 seconds and didn't stick to the pan – you're ready to go! Use about 3 tablespoons of batter per galette and cook one at a time for roughly 30 seconds each side.

4 Place the cooked galettes on a plate in a low oven to keep them warm while you finish cooking the rest.

5 Put the grill on a medium heat and grill your ham until it's crispy, then chop up into little pieces. Keep your pan on, pop a galette back in the pan and on one half of the galette add some cheese, ham and a sprinkle of walnuts. Fold the other side of the galette over. You can flip once if you like – we are just looking to melt the cheese.

TO SERVE

Serve as you like – depending on the size of my pan, I like to make 2–3 big filled galettes per person.

Churros con Chocolate

I've been in love with Spain since I was five years old and they gave me chocolate spread instead of butter, and sorbet in a frozen orange. Churros con chocolate with a big glass of café con leche is heaven in the morning.

Warning: I consider this the most difficult recipe in the book and the least healthy to boot! With the hot oil, have a fire blanket to hand, keep the extractor fan on and only use a few inches of oil to avoid splashes. Oil fires are no craic, so let's not get hurt in the name of a sweet tooth.

Note: I don't use cups for this recipe – it can be temperamental so it needs the precision of grams!

1   Often I'm a little lazy with exact measurements, but this is one recipe where you really need it to be spot on or the batter for the churros just won't work out right.

2   I like to have everything laid out so there's no faffing about later. Have a plate ready with kitchen paper to pop the churros onto when they're out of the oil. Place the topping ingredients in a bowl, mix and have ready for rolling the cooked churros in. Finally, have a big bowl to fill with the finished churros!

3   I usually make the sauce beforehand too. Just break up the chocolate into a bowl and melt in a microwave. For my 700W one, this means on high for 1 minute, a quick stir and then up to 1 minute more. Pour the cream into the melted chocolate and stir vigorously until you get a thick sauce. It'll do this weird thing for a minute or so where it will go all lumpy and weird and pretend not to work, but just keep going. The result is a thick, silky chocolate sauce that you can heat up again later for 20 seconds in the microwave.

MAKES 1 LARGE BOWL TO SHARE AND A CUP (240ML) OF CHOCOLATE SAUCE

For the Topping
½ cup (100g) fine brown sugar
1 tsp cinnamon

For the Sauce
50g good quality milk chocolate *I never use cheap cooking chocolate: that stuff is gross!*
40ml pouring cream

For the Churros
275ml boiling water
150g GF self-raising flour *Doves Farm organic works great for this*
1 tsp sugar
⅓ tsp xanthan gum
2 eggs
50g butter
1 cup (235ml) sunflower oil, for frying

4   Now for the batter. Boil a kettle and measure out the hot water exactly into a jug. Place the flour, sugar and xanthan gum in a bowl and mix well. In a small bowl, whisk up your eggs. Get a small pot on a medium-high heat. When it's nice and hot, pop in the butter. When that's all melted, lash in your water and let it boil away for a few seconds. Take the pot off the heat and chuck in your flour mix. Stirring vigorously, add the eggs. You should get a thick, shiny batter.

5   Fill a piping bag or tube with the batter. I like to use a star-shaped nozzle to get the classic churros shape.

6   Put the cup of sunflower oil in a small pot and make sure to have as much fire-safety back-up as possible (extractor fans, fire blankets, hunky firemen, etc.) Put the oil on a medium-high heat and test after a few minutes with a little teaspoon of the batter. When the oil bubbles and the pastry browns in about 30 seconds, the oil is ready to go! Another clear sign is that the pastry floats to the surface.

7   Use the piping bag/tube to pipe in 5–6cm pieces of dough – they won't be perfect, as Spanish restaurants have fancy machines to do this, but I like when they come out in little twists as well! If the dough is difficult to release from the piping bag, use a sharp knife to cut off the lengths of batter. Cook the churros on both sides for up to 20 seconds each until golden brown. Use a slotted spoon to move them around in the oil and to scoop them out and onto the kitchen paper.

8   When they are done, pop them into the sugar and cinnamon mix and roll them around until fully coated.

9   Repeat the frying and rolling until all the dough is gone.

Fry Not?

In the early days of my coeliac diagnosis, the Sunday fry became a thing of the past. Pudding, sausages, potato cakes and toast? Good luck, mate! With what I had left, people could be forgiven for thinking I was on the Atkins diet – just beans, rashers and a few measly mushrooms. This could not be allowed and the Sunday searches for an exciting fry began.

So here are some of my firm-favourite fry ingredients along with some lovely potatoes, courtesy of my uncle Jimmy, since the Irish can't live without them in a fry. Go on, prove me wrong. Think about it: boxty, potato farls, potato cakes, home fries and hash browns.

SERVES 2 HUNGOVER
HUMANS FOR SUNDAY
BREAKFAST OR AS A HEARTY,
SPEEDY DINNER AFTER A DAY'S
SURFING

4 lovely rashers *smoked Canadian maple are my favourite*

4 GF sausages *Clonakilty ones are amazing*

olive oil, to cook

2 handfuls sliced or chopped mushrooms

salt and pepper

10 large or 15 small cooked new baby potatoes, roughly chopped

pinch dried chilli *less if you don't like it hot*

pinch cayenne pepper

pinch smoked paprika

10 on-the-vine cherry tomatoes (or similar)

1 serving baked beans (page 125) or organic tinned baked beans

pinch ground cinnamon

1   Pop the rashers under the grill on a medium-high heat. I like mine burnt to a crisp, like an Irish person on the first day of a sun holiday, so I have my grill as high as it goes. Pop the sausages on now too.

2   Put a pan on a medium-high heat. When it's hot, pour in a decent glug of oil. We've all heard lots of reasons why it's naughty to fry with olive oil, but this is a Sunday fry not a Monday-morning protein shake – I use olive oil here because I just love the taste!

3   Lash the mushrooms in first, as they take the longest to cook and they need a good bit of olive oil. Season with salt and pepper.

4   Fire the potatoes into the pan beside the mushrooms, adding more oil if needed. Season with the chilli, cayenne and paprika and toss them round a bit. As the potatoes start to brown, add the tomatoes on the vine (hopefully there'll be room).

5   Put the beans in a small pot on a medium-low heat and add a pinch or two of cinnamon for a warm kick. It may sound odd but it gives the classic taste a little zip.

TO SERVE

When everything's
cooked through, serve
up with plenty of toast
(I recommend the Danish
Breakfast Brød on page
34 or the Irish soda-style
bread on page 86), tea and
decent chat – very good
if Sunday is in fact the
'morning after'.

If you're a big protein fan
and need an egg, fry one up
at the very end when the
oil in the pan has absorbed
the lovely flavours of the
spices and tomatoes – a tip
straight from my mammy.

Why I Surf

Lord knows the average member of the surfing community would cringe at my level of skill if they knew how long I've been surfing (or trying to surf). But sure, feck it, it's no one's business but my own. I started surfing as a teenager when my dad moved back to Ireland from London. He figured it was going to be pretty hard to drag a teenager away from all her friends in the metropolis to the sticks in Sligo without some kind of bribe. So I received a week of surf lessons and the rest, as they say, is history. I was hooked from day one and spent an entire summer saving for my first surfboard. Since then surfing, surf clubs and random surf trips have been the source of some of my best friends, best adventures and worst bruises. I'm in the sea most days now, and surfing for me is so many things: it's exercise, stress relief, fun, adrenaline and something great to do with friends. I've found that when living in cities, drinking and socialising can often become people's main post-work pastime, which makes me very sad indeed. Post-surf beers, however, are probably the best you will ever taste!

F3

Surf Playlist

These are just a few of the songs I would listen to
with the gang when we went for surf trips back
in our college days in Galway — Chilled being the
playlist for the way home and Excited for when we
were getting riled up to get in the water.

♥ EXCITED ♥

Adventure Club – 'Retro City', 'Need Your Heart'

Knife Party – 'Internet Friends', 'Bonfire'

The Bloody Beetroots – 'Warp 1.9'

Avicii – 'Levels'

♥ CHILLED ♥

A Flock of Seagulls – 'I Ran (So Far Away)'

Wye Oak – 'Civilian'

Donavon Frankenreiter – 'Shine'

Jack Johnson – 'Banana Pancakes'

Damian Marley – 'And Be Loved'

Snack Attack

A few speedy little snacks

that are perfect for a quick nibble:

1

Slices of banana topped with peanut butter and a smidgen of honey.

2

Apple slices with cheese

3

DIY trail mix: almonds, pumpkin seeds, macadamia nuts, dried cranberries and banana chips

4

Simple chia pudding: 2–3 tbsp chia seeds and ⅔ cup (160ml) chocolate-flavoured coconut milk (the more chia the thicker the pud); mix well and leave overnight. I like to top it with berries and some toasted desiccated coconut

5

Umami seeds: toast (dry fry) a cup or so (140g) of sunflower seeds in a pan, pop them in a glass jar while they're still hot and add a tablespoon or two of tamari soy sauce. Instant salty, crunchy snack.

Lu

nch

Midday meals are often less of a hazard when you're cooking gluten free. With rice noodles, corn pasta and potatoes, carbs ain't a problem. It's when it comes to entertaining people or eating out that the gluten dodging starts.

I'm a big advocate of nailing down the basics first. For example, if you get a handle on one of the bread recipes, make it on a Sunday. You can slice the entire loaf and freeze it in pairs of slices. Then make one of the delish soups in this section and portion it out – check your local Asian market for take-away sized tubs: they're a godsend. Now you're sorted for a week of lunches!

Another handy tip is bagels. I recently went on a weekend trip to Oslo with one of my surfer girls. Everyone was harping on about how expensive the place would be so we decided to make handbag-sized lunches. The key ingredient? GF bagels. Get them in your local supermarket and fill with your fave ingredients. They hold together a lot better than commercial gluten-free bread. And who doesn't like bread that looks like a giant Polo mint? My personal numero uno is low-fat cream cheese, smoked salmon and a little cracked black pepper. It seemed to go with the Norwegian fascination with preserved fish ...

Breads

Gluten-free cake can be delicious and easy, but GF bread is a whole different story. These two breads are my duo of joy after many years of enduring sawdusty gluten-free bread. I highly recommend making these loaves in batches, letting them cool and then freezing them in portioned slices so you always have some to hand for breakfasts, soups and mopping up delicious sauces.

No-Amish-Beard-Required Corn Bread

On a trip to Salem a few years ago, I discovered that bread could literally make people go crazy. Yes, bread mould was at the heart of the witch trials! I got to thinking about those peculiar pilgrims and their affinity for making stuff from scratch. Maybe it was time to ditch the sawdust GF bread and have a crack at making my own. The result? A fluffy, melt-in-the-mouth cornbread that works well as a savoury with soups or, if lathered with butter and jam, as a sweet with tea. Yum.

1   Preheat the oven to 200°C.

2   Grease your chosen pan (I use a 23cm round skillet) with some butter.

3   Mix all the dry bowl ingredients together. Mix all the wet bowl ingredients together.

4   Make a well (a hole) in the middle of the dry mix. Now pour the wet mix into the well. Use a wooden spoon to slowly stir in the dry mix from the edges till it's all combined with the wet mix.

5   Pour the mix into the greased pan and pop it in the oven for 20–30 minutes. My oven is a bit wonky so it takes about 25 minutes. You know the bread's done when it's golden brown on top and a toothpick or fork popped into it comes out clean.

TO SERVE

Once it has cooled a little, put a big plate over the pan like a lid and flip it. Tah-dah! Lovely bread. Gobble immediately for best results.

---

1 ROUND LOAF MAKES ABOUT 16 SLICES

Dry Bowl

1½ cups (240g) cornmeal *the coarse yellow stuff, not the cornflour that's used to thicken soups*

½ cup (60g) ground almonds

1 tsp salt – I use pink Himalayan

2 tsp GF baking powder

Wet Bowl

4 tbsp butter – plus extra for the pan

1½ cups (375g) yogurt *I use Glenisk natural yogurt, as it has a slightly bitter kick; this can also be subbed with buttermilk for a more classic recipe*

3 tbsp maple syrup

Irish-Mammy-Approved Country Soda Bread

I love, love, love this recipe. I think it's my favourite bread. It tastes just like the Irish classic and can be cut with a proper serrated bread knife (unlike most gluten-free bread). It goes perfectly with eggs for breakfast, all the soups in this section or solo, slathered with butter and washed down with a cup of tea.

MAKES 1 SMALL ROUND LOAF (IT'S BEST EATEN FRESH) – DOUBLE THE QUANTITY FOR A BIG FELLA

1 ½ cups (250g) Doves Farm GF self-raising flour

1 tsp bread soda

½ tsp GF baking powder

big pinch of salt

½ cup (50g) milled linseeds

1 cup (230ml) buttermilk

1 tsp honey

1 egg

1 Preheat the oven to 230°C.

2 Sift the flour, bread soda and baking powder into a big bowl. Then lash in the salt and milled linseeds. Give it a quick stir.

3 In a jug, whisk up the buttermilk, honey and egg – try to get as much air in as possible.

4 Science-y bit: soda bread rises because of the chemical reaction between the base – the soda – and the acid – the buttermilk. This reaction gets to work the second the two meet. So, with this in mind, it's good to have your baking tray with a slip of baking parchment ready to go.

5 Make a well in the centre of the dry mix and pour in the wet mix from the jug. Incorporate the lot with your hands. I make a claw shape with my right hand and imitate an electric mixer. If the dough is a little dry add some more buttermilk; if it's a bit wet add a little more flour.

6 Scoop the dough up, shape roughly into a ball with your hands and plonk it down on the baking tray. Cut an X across the top and into the oven it goes! Bake at 230°C for 5 minutes. This forms the lovely crust. Then reduce the heat to 200°C for 15–20 minutes – 20 minutes gives a nice coffee-brown colour, just how I like it. When it's done, take it out and let it cool completely on a wire rack before slicing.

Soups

I feel quick, tasty soups – or at least the ones I make – are
variations on a theme, the basic elements of which are:

1
Big lumbering 'carby' veg
e.g. potatoes

2
Smaller tasty veg
e.g. parsnips

3
Allium-type yoke
onion/shallot/garlic

4
**A trustworthy but taste- packed
GF stock**
Knorr Stock Pots are lovely

5
Kick-ass flavour enhancer
fresh herbs or spices

6
Healthy fats
*such as coconut oil, real butter
or olive oil*

7
Snazzy-looking topping
*(only required to impress guests … or
yourself if you're having a rough day)
toasted seeds, more fresh herbs, crispy
fried shallots, paprika salt, dollop of
Greek yogurt*

I never put cabbage-type things in my soups as they can go bitter when you leave 'em on for a bit to boil. Also I tend to make my soups dairy free and vegan for the most part so as many folks as possible can eat them!

I used to think when you read things like 'roasted squash soup' on menus that the chefs were being super fancy. Recently I've discovered that roasting the veg first is Pure. Unadulterated. Laziness. And I love it! While it may seem like extra time and work, roasting all your veg in advance means a) you don't have to peel them and b) you don't have to cut them up into tiny chunks. Say goodbye to grated fingers and tennis elbow!

Funny thing is, I don't often go for soups in restaurants – I'm generally suspicious of whether the stock is really GF and I don't like having unknown quantities of cream being poured into my body. So the recipes here are my absolute favourite homemade soups. I tend to make the 'meatier' ones in the winter, and, realistically, I even have the heartier veg ones in the summer – it's Ireland, people, you never know what it will be like!

Lean and Green Courgette Soup

When we have guests in the Gyreum Ecolodge, there's nothing better than being able to tell them the food came straight from the garden. When there was an insane amount of courgettes a few years back – and we were getting nervous twitches at the thought of eating any more stuffed ones – on my mama's recommendation I decided to try them out in a soup. This recipe might seem a little Plain-Jane to look at but it's mad tasty and also mad good for you!

SERVES 4–6 VEGOPHILES

1 white onion

2 stalks celery *nick the top and bottom and do your best to pull out the stringy bits: they are not so nice in smooth soups!*

3 large Rooster potatoes

2 large courgettes *or 4 'supermarket sized' ones: the smaller they are the tastier!*

olive oil for frying – roughly 1 tbsp

2 cups (480ml) GF veggie stock

salt and pepper to taste

1   Chop up all your veg whatever way you like – we are going to blend the bejaysus out of them later so it doesn't matter too much what size they are.

2   Get a nice big pot for your soup and lash it on a medium-high heat. When the pot is hot (hey, that rhymes!) pour in your splash of olive oil and a little piece of onion. If it sizzles you're good to chuck in the rest of the onion. Toss in the celery and stir until the onions turn translucent.

3   Next add your potatoes. My mom is the queen of tasty soups and at this point she would turn the heat down and put a lid on the pot to let the potatoes 'sweat' a bit, for about 5 minutes. If you know your pot is really crap, though, don't do it, as the onions might burn!

4   Add your chopped courgette and stock. When I'm being super-organised, I have the stock in a jug, all mixed, hot and raring to go by the time the veggies are ready. Half-cover your pot and simmer till the potatoes are soft – usually about 30 minutes.

5   Blend the soup until smooth with a hand blender – be careful not to splash your lovely clothes with hot soup (I've done this so many times). If you like a thinner soup, add a little more hot water.

6   Add salt and pepper to taste. I like tons of pepper.

TO SERVE

This goes lovely with a dollop of natural yogurt in the middle and a sprig of parsley. Go-Go-Gadget green healthy soup!

TOP TIPS

I have no idea why people don't say this more, but don't add the salt and pepper till the very end. Since you will lose water as the soup simmers down, it can end up too salty and peppery and it can also affect the flavour of the veg!

White Winter-Veg Soup

The Snow White of soups! I made this one day because I simply got bored of eating soups that were sort-of-orange or sort-of-green. This is a lovely curl-up-by-the-fire kind of soup and I really hope you try it with the nutmeg as I think it makes the dish!

MAKES ENOUGH FOR 5
WEEKDAY WINTER LUNCHES

4 large Rooster potatoes

1 turnip or celeriac when it's in season

5 parsnips *3 if they are massive*

2 stalks celery *nick the top and bottom and do your best to pull out the stringy bits, which are not so nice in smooth soups!*

1 large white onion

olive oil for frying

4 cups (950ml) GF vegetable stock

pinch nutmeg or allspice

1 tsp honey

salt and pepper to taste

1   Peel the potatoes, turnip and parsnips and cut into small chunks. Normally I'm not a believer in peeling veg – I just give them a good scrub – but this is a rawther refined-looking soup, so give it a go!

2   De-string the celery and slice 'em up. Peel and finely chop your onions. Out of a strange habit, I always prep onions last and cook them first.

3   Put a large pot on the stove at a medium-high heat. When you reckon it's nice and hot, glug in a bit of olive oil and a piece of onion. If it sizzles, add the rest of your onion and sauté away!

4   When the onions are translucent, chuck in the rest of your veg and give it a good stir. Add your stock, spice and honey. Reduce the heat, half-cover the pot and let simmer until the veggies are soft. This can take up to 40 minutes or even longer, as the parsnips and the turnip can be slow boilers!

5   Blend the soup with a hand blender and season with salt and pepper.

TO SERVE

This soup is lovely as it is, but sometimes I add some toasted seeds on top for a bit of crunch!

Disco Barbie Beetroot Soup

I don't care what people say: it is completely possible to be a tomboy and a girly girl. I love this soup, as it reminds me of the Barbie pink of my little girl days – when you could find me up a tree, covered in mud, in a pink dress with frilly white socks and little patent leather shoes. The decadent shade of this soup comes from fresh beetroots, and you might want to wear gloves while you prep them so you don't look like an NCIS extra. Also, I implore you, please, please, please don't use cooked vacuum-packed beets – they just aren't the same!

1   Peel the beetroot. You might want to wear rubber gloves and use a non-favourite plastic chopping board for this, as it can be pretty messy. Roughly chop the beetroot, carrots, onion and celery.

2   Put a good, large non-stick pot on a medium-high heat. When it's hot, lash in a glug of olive oil and chuck all of the veggies in. That's right – all of them. No fancy sautéing. Cover with a lid and let them steam away to their hearts' content. After 10 minutes, if it's freaking you out a bit that you're not doing anything, give it a little stir. Reduce the heat a bit and cover again. Let the veggies hang out this way for about 30 minutes.

3   When the veggies are soft, lash in the beans and stock. Cook away for about 10 minutes. Take off the heat, blend with a hand blender and season to taste!

TO SERVE

This awesomely bright soup is lovely with a dollop of crème fraiche and a bit of greenery on top – I tend to use parsley.

MAKES ENOUGH FOR 5 NEON-COLOURED LUNCHES

3 uncooked beetroots

6 carrots

1 red onion

2 sticks celery *nick the top and bottom and do your best to pull out the stringy bits, which are not nice in smooth soups*

olive oil

400g tinned mixed beans, drained and rinsed *this thickens the soup, like potato, but adds a little more protein*

4 cups (950ml) GF vegetable stock

salt and pepper to taste

Disco Barbie Beetroot Soup, page 93

Mysteriously Mexican Soup

This is my favourite soup – minimal effort, maximum taste. It came about because I had a gammy shoulder from a surfing injury and chopping vegetables really irritated it. Eureka! The ingredients I was playing around with felt more Indian and North American, but when it was all cooked up it had a rich Mexican and mysteriously meaty flavour!

MAKES 1 BIG POT TO LIVE OFF ON WEEKDAYS

½ a massive sweet potato or 1 normal sized *I say this because the ones in my supermarket always seem to be huge*

1 butternut squash

1 clove garlic

1 large red onion *which is actually purple and also called a French onion (it's having an identity crisis)*

1 tbsp virgin olive oil

1 tsp turmeric

½ tsp smoked paprika

1 tsp sweet paprika *sometimes called pimenton*

squidge of tomato purée – roughly a tbsp

400g tinned chopped tomatoes *plain, not with herbs*

2 cups (500ml) GF vegetable stock

To Serve

crème fraiche

fresh coriander (cilantro) leaves

paprika salt *yeah, that's just half-salt and half-paprika mixed together and put into a salt grinder*

lime wedge

1 Preheat your oven to 180°C. Make sure there isn't an oven tray in there baking away all lonely.

2 Lay out your sweet potato, squash, garlic and onion on a baking tray. I leave everything whole except the onion, which I cut in half but leave the skin on. I usually lash on a few extra cloves of garlic, in case one burns or you want to use them for a salad dressing or dip like the ones on pages 284 and 286.

3 Pop the lot in the oven for 30–45 mins, depending on what your oven's like. Kick back and relax for a wee bit. This is usually where I get distracted and start cooking something else, so set a timer if you don't trust yourself: charcoaled veg aren't ideal.

4 When the roast veg are done (they should be soft enough that a fork slides through them), set them aside to cool a bit and pop on the kettle with about 1 litre of water in it.

5 Depending on the toughness of your hands (I've scary weight-lifty asbestos hands), you can start peeling the skin off your veg. Scoop the seeds out of the squash and discard. You won't need to chop anything, as it will all mush away happily in the pot.

6   On the stove, heat up a big pot. Add the olive oil when it's nice and hot.
    I like to add the turmeric and paprika at this point, as the soup is more
    flavourful when you add the spices to the oil at the start. Add the roast
    veg and the squidge of tomato purée. Move these lads around for a bit
    and then add the tinned tomatoes and stock.

7   Let the soup simmer for up to 30 minutes – it doesn't need much longer
    as most of your ingredients were already cooked. When it has cooled
    a little, use a hand blender to create a smooth soup. You can add more
    water at this point if you prefer a thinner consistency.

TO SERVE
Place a big dollop of crème fraiche in the middle, sprinkle with fresh
coriander, paprika salt and a squeeze of lime.

TOP TIP
For extra protein and texture you could add a tin of pinto or black beans after
blending the soup and then pop it back on the heat for a few more minutes
before serving.

Thai Not? Carrot, Coriander and Coconut Soup

Carrot soup is a family favourite and we always make it with either coriander or almonds. It works really well if you sub the coriander for fresh ginger, but my favourite is this Thai-inspired version with coconut, coriander seeds and fresh coriander.

MAKES 3 BIG SERVINGS OR 4 WITH SOME SIDES

6 big carrots – scrubbed but not peeled

1 large Rooster potato

1 large white onion

2 stalks celery – with the stringy bits taken off

1 tbsp crushed coriander seeds *much nicer if you do this yourself instead of using the powder*

olive oil

3½ cups (800ml) GF vegetable or chicken stock

400ml tinned coconut milk

handful fresh coriander leaves, to garnish

lime wedge, for squeezing over

1   Roughly chop your carrots, potato, onion and celery – big chunks are fine. Crush the coriander seeds using a mortar and pestle. If you don't have a set, no prob – just put the seeds in a sandwich bag and crush with something heavy, e.g. a rolling pin or the tin of coconut milk.

2   Put a big pot on a medium-high heat. When the pot is hot, dry fry your crushed coriander seeds. When you're getting a lovely smell and the coriander has browned a little, pop it on a plate and put to one side. Put the pot back on the heat and glug in a tablespoon of olive oil. Throw in a piece of onion – if it sizzles the pot is hot! Chuck in all your veg, stir around a bit to coat in oil and pop the coriander back in.

3   Now reduce the heat a little, stick the lid on the pot and leave it there to sweat like a naughty kid outside the principal's office. After 10 minutes give it a stir and a check. Let it stew away for another 20 minutes. When the veggies are soft (you can easily slide a knife through them), add your stock.

4   Take the soup off the heat and blend with a hand blender. Add a tin of coconut milk and put back on the stove if this has reduced the temperature (I don't like my soup too hot, so I am usually happy with it as is).

TO SERVE
Top your soup bowls with
fresh coriander leaves and
a slice of lime on the side.
This can also be lovely with a
sprinkle of some crushed salted
peanuts and beansprouts.

TOP TIP
Use $\frac{1}{2}$ cup (60g) ground
almonds instead of the coriander
seeds, if they're not your thing.

Salads

I wasn't always a fan of salad. I figured it was a sign that
I was in my mid-twenties when I finally started making
salad for myself. Really what it was, though, was finally
understanding that salads could be more than a sad bit of
iceberg lettuce with a slimy sauce on top. Here are some
of my go-to options. They work great in a lunchbox for
carting around on your adventures!

The Ariel Special – Prawn Soba Noodle Salad

With the great mix of protein, complex carbs and all the minerals from the seaweed, this dish is perfect fuel for ocean adventures. This is a lovely fresh salad so there isn't too much cooking involved.

1   Rehydrate the seaweed by placing it in a bowl of hot water for five minutes.

2   Put all the ingredients for the dressing in a clean glass jar and shake till it's all combined. Try it and adjust according to your own taste. This is a democracy, people!

3   Lash on a pot of water to boil. Follow the instructions on your buckwheat noodle pack, but I find they usually take between 5 and 10 minutes. I go for less time so they don't go soggy. When the noodles are done, strain and rinse them and toss them with a little oil so they don't stick together. Leave them to cool while you prep the rest of the bits for the salad.

4   Pat the seaweed dry and slice it, the cucumber and the spring onions into thin strips. Slice the prawns in half lengthways.

TO SERVE

Portion out your noodles and arrange the rest of the salad ingredients as you like with the dressing on the side for folks to help themselves!

SERVES 2 HUMANS PRETENDING TO BE MER-PEOPLE

3 strips dried alaria seaweed

2 portions soba noodles *check they are 100% buckwheat to ensure GF-ness*

⅓ cucumber

2 spring onions

200g cooked and peeled prawns

1 tbsp salted and roasted peanuts, crushed

1 tbsp black sesame seeds, toasted

For the Dressing

1 tbsp toasted sesame seed oil

1 tbsp tamari GF soy sauce

2 tbsp lime juice

1 tsp honey

1 tsp grated ginger root

pepper to taste *there's already salt in the tamari*

2 tbsp sunflower oil, optional *if you like your dressing a little less tangy and a little more oily*

She Sells Seashells by the Seashore – Cockle Salsa Salad

In my cupboard I usually have a few tins of sustainably caught tuna and a tin of sardines in tomato sauce for those emergency no-grocery days. But these last few months I've fallen for cockles in brine. It's always nice to shake things up a little – these little fellas are a fantastic low-fat protein source and you can sing that song about Molly Malone while you're prepping.

SERVES 2, WITH SOME OTHER SALADS AND A SLAB OF TORTILLA, OR 1 ALL BY ITSELF

½ small red onion or ¼ big one

½ lemon or 1 lime, juice only

90g (drained weight) tinned cockles in brine *you could use tuna if you like, but it doesn't pack the same punch*

10 cherry tomatoes

1 tbsp balsamic vinegar

glug of olive oil *I use lots, 3–4 tbsp: sure, it's good for your skin*

salt and pepper to taste

1   Finely dice your red onion – the finer the better. For me onions should be tasted but not felt: it gives me the heebie-jeebies to bite into a piece of raw onion.

2   In a bowl, cover your diced red onion with the lemon or lime juice. This takes away the raw-oniony kick. The juice also turns pink, so it makes a cool-looking dressing. If you have time leave these in the fridge for a half hour or so.

3   Drain your cockles and pop them in the salad bowl. Cut the cherry tomatoes in half and chuck them in too.

4   Pop in the onion and lemon-juice mix. Add the balsamic vinegar, olive oil and salt and pepper to taste.

TO SERVE

This is really tasty garnished with some fresh herbs. If you'd like your salad to go a little further you could add some greenery, my favourite being rocket and baby leaf spinach for a good nutritional kick. For some extra carbs, I have this dish with roasted sweet potatoes. Just roast the potato in its skin, no oil or anything! It takes about 30–40 minutes so, before prepping the salad, I pop a few in so I have extra left over for later meals.

Sunny Summer Quinoa Salad

There are lots of little bits to this salad – but, oh my God, it's so good. I use this quantity either as a main event at a summer lunch or I keep it portioned in the fridge to take out with me.

1   Give the quinoa a good rinse with cold water to stop it getting a bitter taste as it cooks (due to a coating on the outside of the grain). I do this in a sieve, since the quinoa grains are itty-bitty and they fall out of a colander.

2   Add the quinoa, stock and bay leaf or leaves to a pot and bring to the boil. I don't tend to add salt as I find the stock is usually salty enough by itself. Lower the heat and simmer for 15 minutes with the lid on. I find my stove works best on a lower setting with the lid on – if it's too high the quinoa can bubble over. After this, I take a teeny bit out and have a nibble. If it's done (cooked through and no gritty feeling) I take the quinoa off the heat and let it stand for 5 minutes with the lid on to fluffy-ise itself. In theory, you would let this cool down, go off on your merry way and come back later when it was cool to complete the salad. But I'm usually hungry, so that doesn't tend to happen.

3   Slice the onion into super-thin strips and soak them in the lemon juice. This takes the raw-onion-esque whack off them (and colours the lemon juice pink, which looks cool in the salad). Slice the peppers into long thin strips. Cut the grapes in half lengthways.

4   Find a lovely big salad bowl – I love the turned wooden ones – and layer up the salad: quinoa first (don't forget to take out the bay leaf), then chicken, grapes and veggies. Chuck the lemon juice on with the onions and sprinkle over the coriander, dried cranberries and toasted seeds. Follow with the olive oil and a little salt and pepper to taste.

SERVES 3 OR 2 RAVENOUS HUMANS

1 cup (185g) uncooked quinoa

2 cups (470ml) GF vegetable stock

1 fresh or 2 dried bay leaves

½ red onion

1 tbsp lemon juice *more if you like extra zip!*

2 bell peppers, sliced *I use yellow mostly, for some reason I can't stand the green ones*

1 cup (170g) green seedless grapes

300g cooked tikka masala chicken *I get Green Farm as it uses certified GF seasoning!*

¼ cup (25g) fresh coriander leaves, chopped

3 tbsp craisins *dried cranberries, not crazy raisins*

4 tbsp toasted seeds *I use sunflower and pumpkin*

2 tbsp olive oil

salt and pepper to taste

Sunny Summer Quinoa Salad, page 103

Sexy-Skin Roast Veggie Salad

This is an ode to those lustrous-looking Mediterraneans and their wonderful skin! I abuse my skin mightily by chucking it in the sea every week and blasting it with the salt and wind of the Atlantic, so this salad is a great way of getting in the healthy fats that keep skin happy. It's also a great throw-together when you've suddenly got a big gang to feed and have a lot of cupboard staples (like the chickpeas and the quinoa) and long-range veg (things that last for ages) to be used up.

SERVES 4 AS A SIDE OR MORE
IF ONE OF A SELECTION OF
SALADS

1 cup (185g) quinoa

2 cups (470ml) GF vegetable stock

1 fresh or 2 dried bay leaves

1 large aubergine

olive oil

1 tbsp tamari soy sauce

1 red onion, cut in half

1 large red pepper

200g tinned chickpeas or red kidney beans, drained and rinsed

4 big handfuls of baby leaf spinach, washed

2 tbsp lemon juice

salt and pepper to taste

1   Preheat the oven to 200°C.

2   Pop the quinoa in a sieve and give it a good rinse with cold water to stop it getting a bitter taste as it cooks.

3   Add the quinoa, stock and bay leaf or leaves to a pot and bring to the boil. I don't tend to add salt as I find the stock cube/pot is usually salty enough by itself. Lower the heat and simmer for 15 minutes with the lid on. After this, have a little nibble. If it's done (cooked through and no gritty feeling) take it off the heat and leave it aside to cool with the lid on.

4   Cut the aubergine into long strips about 1cm thick. In a bowl, toss them with 2 tablespoons of olive oil and 1 of tamari soy sauce.

5   Grease a baking tray with a little olive oil and lay out the onion halves, the aubergine slices and the whole red pepper. That's right, stalk and all! The pepper roasts in a lovely way when whole, but it goes kind of sad and dry if you do it in individual slices. Roast for 15 mins, then swish the aubergines around a bit so they bake evenly and turn the pepper over. They're done when the aubergine slices are soft and have reduced in size and when the pepper is soft and a little blackened on the outside. The onions should be soft and the top a little crispy. Leave them aside to cool.

6   Put the cooked quinoa and the chickpeas in a big salad bowl. Throw in the aubergine. Remove the outer skin of the onion if you haven't already and slice into long pieces. Cut the top off the pepper, scrape out the seeds using a spoon and cut into slices. Add the pepper and onion to the salad bowl. Add the spinach to the bowl and drizzle with a tablespoon of olive oil and lemon juice. Season with salt and pepper. Toss the whole salad well – the warmth of the veg will wilt the spinach.

TO SERVE

This salad is good to go while still a little warm, and it also keeps well in the fridge for several days. I tend to serve it as a side or with a selection of other salads, as it can be a bit rich on its own.

All the Other Tasty Lunch Stuff

These are all the essentials that are not soups, salads or breads – a tasty assortment inspired by my travels and the changing seasons.

Brie, Cranberry and Stuffing Sambo

This is a classic bold sandwich, to my mind – something you might get when you're running around like a headless chicken doing Christmas shopping and you want to give yourself a little treat. I've yet to see this version in any restaurant, since decent gluten-free breadcrumbs are hard to come by. But if you're a big fan (as I am) it's well worth the little bit of effort to make it yourself. Have it around the time you're making stuffing for a chicken or Christmas turkey so you don't feel like you're going through a massive palaver for one dish!

Gluten-free bread is often best toasted, so toast or grill the bread. Butter your slices, lay the slices of Brie on the bottom slice, top with stuffing, then turkey and finally cranberry sauce and the top slice. Voilà, you're ready to go!

TO SERVE

If you want to treat yourself even more, put the Brie on one of the slices of bread as you toast it. Then enter melted cheese heaven …

SERVES 1 FESTIVE HUMAN

2 slices of your favourite GF bread

butter, for spreading

3 big slices Brie

4 tbsp Rosemary Stuffing (page 266)

turkey or chicken slices if you're not vegetarian

4 tbsp Cranberry Sauce (page 295)

Saucy Spanish Tortilla

I've lived in Spain a few times now and it was quickly apparent that the only healthy gluten-free breakfast option was tortilla. The Spanish do wonderful gluten-free pastries but, like I said, healthy option. There are so many variations that it never gets boring, and with its eggy protein, potatoey carbohydrates and Mediterranean-olive-oily fats, it's a great way to fuel yourself for the day. This recipe is one I liked to make during my college days. It worked equally well in the evening if I had a late lecture, as it gives sustained energy without the carb sleepies you get from pasta.

SERVES 2 BUDGET-CONSCIOUS HUNGRY HUMANS

4 eggs

splash of milk

salt and pepper

2 large shallots or 1 small white onion

6 large cooked new baby potatoes *these guys cook fast and keep their shape when boiled*

olive oil

2 cloves garlic, crushed

grated cheese (optional)

1   Crack the eggs into a large bowl (watch out for shell!) along with a dash of milk, and season with salt and pepper. Mix well. You can leave out the milk if you want your recipe dairy free.

2   Finely dice the onion – some people like bigger chunks of onion but, personally, I like to 'taste their flavour, not feel their presence'.

3   Slice the potatoes up nice and thin – about $1/2$cm or less a slice – or chop into 1cm cubes. This is a great way to use up cooked potatoes when you've some left over after dinner.

4   Heat up a good non-stick pan on a medium-high heat. Non-stick is the name of the game, people – crappy old pans make for sad, burnt tortilla. When it's nice and hot add a glug of olive oil. Throw in a little bit of onion to test – when it sizzles, add the rest of the onion and sauté for a few minutes until it looks less pale. Add the garlic and cook for a few more minutes.

5   Take the onion and garlic out and put on a plate to one side. Add more olive oil to the pan and layer in the potato slices and the onion/garlic mix.

6   Pour over the egg mixture and push the potatoes around a bit to get the egg mix right in there (like swimwear!).

7   Put the grill on a medium heat. When the tortilla has begun to solidify in the pan (doesn't look as wet on top) take it off the heat and grate cheese over it (only if you want to, of course). Then pop the pan under the grill – careful to keep the handle out so it doesn't melt. Take it out when the cheese has bubbled and the tortilla is a nice golden colour. You need to watch it here, as this happens quickly.

TO SERVE

If it's for breakfast, serve Spanish style with freshly squeezed orange juice, some bread and olive oil and salt for dipping on the side. This can also be a great snack if you've got friends over in the evening – served cut into cubes with cocktail sticks, it goes well with a cold beer (for gluten friendlies) or a dry white wine (for the GFs)! If you don't like it plain you can sauce it up – I like Mojo sauce, a Canarian favourite, or the Park restaurant near my Airbnb in Santa Cruz served it with garlic mayo. Yum!

Jose's Game-Changing Chicken Wrap

A few years ago I and some of my best friends decided to live in America for the summer. We worked in surf schools and beach clubs and teased the lads for being cabana boys. With the joys of skint travel, we lived in an apartment with a strange little grill oven and a stove that was more interested in gassing us to death than cooking anything. So most of our food had to be bought on the hoof. It's pretty scary for a coeliac to be reliant on the outside world for daily meals and I did get poisoned once in NY. But my absolute favourite place to shop was a little Mexican grocer's around the corner. You may notice the theme of Mexican food in this book – it's because Mexico has one of the most naturally gluten-free diets in the world, since it's based around veg, meat, beans, corn and rice! We loved chatting to the owner about food, weather – everything really – while he made up the delicious wraps and we drooled watching. I've tried many different ingredient combos since then and still think his is the winner! In Ireland I've only been able to source multigrain GF wraps, which are lovely but not that big. If you're in a country where you can get the big corn tortillas, you're a lucky duck. Please send me some.

Makes 1~2 wraps, depending on the size

1 big free-range chicken breast *happy chickens taste better and are better for you*

olive oil, for roasting

salt and pepper

1 red bell pepper

½ avocado

½ ball low-fat mozzarella

1–2 GF tortilla wraps *the bigger the better*

handful baby leaf spinach

For the Dressing

¼ cup (60ml) olive oil

¼ cup (60ml) balsamic vinegar

salt and pepper

2 cloves raw garlic or 3 roasted

1   Preheat the oven to 180°C.

2   Pop the chicken breast into a small baking dish, drizzle with a little olive oil and season with salt and pepper. Pop the whole pepper on its own dish and rub it with a little olive oil. Put the cloves of garlic for the dressing in with the pepper (with their skin still on). Roast garlic is even nicer than raw in the dressing and easier for your stomach to digest too! Lash both dishes in the oven. Cook the chicken for up to 30 minutes or until white the whole way through. The pepper will only take about 20 minutes (turn over once after 10 minutes) so remember to take it out early.

3   When the pepper is blackened a little and nice and soft it's done. Jose used to peel the peppers, but I like the blackened bits of skin on the outside. Cut off the top of the pepper and scrape out the seeds with a spoon. Cut the flesh into rough chunks.

4   Cut the avocado into long strips. Finely slice the mozzarella.

5   I like to 'refresh' the GF wraps for about 20 seconds on high in the microwave and then lay them out on a big sheet of tinfoil on a plate.

6   Slice the chicken breast and line it along the centre of the wrap. Add the avocado, peppers, spinach and mozzarella. If the wrap is small, I just use half the pepper; if it's a big'un, I use the lot for extra vegness!

7   I like to make a jar of the dressing so I can use it for other salads as well. Simply mix the oil and vinegar and then season with salt and pepper. If you're using roasted garlic, remove the skins, crush and add. If using raw garlic, chop 2 cloves into quarters and mix them in. The dressing will get more deliciously garlicky the longer it sits – just be careful not to pour the big chunks of garlic onto anything later!

TO SERVE

Jose used to wrap it all up at this point, chop it in half and give us little containers of the dressing to pour over the halves as we ate them. This trick also stops the wrap getting soggy if you're taking it to work or college with you. It's delicious even without the dressing, but I'd totally encourage you to try it.

This wrap is high in healthy fats from the avocado and olive oil. If you're watching your calorie intake, ensure the cheese is low fat and sub in a tasty green leaf like rocket instead of the avocado.

TOP TIPS

If you need to cut out dairy, simply leave out the mozzarella, as the avocado is perfectly creamy by itself!

This is a fantastic weekday lunch staple – simply prepare a big batch of chicken and roasted peppers on a Sunday and make up the wraps cold during the week. For shear unadulterated yumminess, if you have a panini press or toasty maker, you could press the wrap, toasting the outside and melting the cheese!

Surf Instructor's Club Sambo

Club sandwiches weren't always a major player for me, but I know from talking to other folks who've gone GF that it's something that has been sorely missed. GF sliced breads are usually not enough to manage the heft of the club sambo ingredients. Simple answer? Use a bagel! GF bagels are far more advanced in their technology compared to the sliced pan. For the middle slice of your sambo just shave the top and bottom (tee hee) off a second bagel. You can keep those for a slimbo sambo the next day if you're feeling guilty. As for the ingredients, it's a mix of clubs from various beloved cafés and hotels around Ireland. The first rule of club sambo ... This is always great for a big feed after a surf or teaching a lesson.

SERVES 1 HUMAN, MULTIPLY INGREDIENTS AS THE PARTY REQUIRES

2 GF bagels

2 slices bacon *leave out for vegetarian*

½ ripe avocado

1 egg

sunflower oil, for frying

butter, for spreading *use an olive-oil spread for dairy free*

free-range mayonnaise, for spreading *remember, mayo is dairy free: there is often confusion there*

1 slice tinned pineapple

1 Slice 1 bagel in half, slice the other in 3 and just keep the middle bit for now.

2 Put your grill on a medium-high heat. Put the bagel slices and bacon on a grill tray and under the grill.

3 Slice up the avocado. Fry the egg in a pan with a little sunflower oil. You could poach it instead for damage control, but I wouldn't be that bothered myself.

4 When the bagels are toasted and the bacon is grilled to your required level of incineration, butter/mayo all your slices and stack them up!

5 The order I go with – to stop stuff falling out of the bottom bagel hole – is: bottom bagel; bacon; avocado; middle bagel; egg; pineapple; top bagel.

TO SERVE

I personally hate lettuce in club sambos, but go right ahead if it's important to you! These look great sliced in half and plated up with a big pile of crisps and washed down with a mug of tea.

Canadian Boxing Day Lunch Sandwich

Family lore tells me that this is a classic Canuck lunch for the day after Christmas when you don't have any designs on cooking and will probably just veg for the whole day watching _Die Hard_ in a fluffy onesie. This one was off the cards for me for a few years until I finally figured out how to make stuffing GF and found a decent gravy!

SERVES 2 LAZY NON-COOKERS

1½ cups (350ml) hot GF gravy _a premix one or the insanely tasty mushroom one on page 168_

4 slices GF bread

butter, for buttering

1 cup (1 big handful) rosemary stuffing (page 266) _or lots more if you're a stuffing fiend_

1 cup (125g) chopped cooked turkey (or roast chicken) pieces

1 The Canadian side of my family tells me that you are not allowed to serve the sandwich any other way than this.

2 Get your gravy on, and make sure it's hot, since it is meant to be a big 'bringer of heat' to the rest of the sambo. Toast your bread – so it holds its shape better once it's drowning in gravy.

3 Layers go like this from the bottom up for each sandwich: slice of toast; butter; stuffing; slice of toast; chicken or turkey; drown with gravy.

TO SERVE

Don't mess with it – it's perfect! Also don't worry about trying to make it healthy – it's essentially a stuffed-crust pizza, stuffed with bread and with gravy instead of cheese.

Oh, Mon Dieu, French Toast

For a long time GF bread didn't hold together well enough to even make it worthwhile to bother making French toast. It was more like French chunks, which just sounds kind of weird. Now that things have improved a bit, this works well with any supermarket GF sliced loaf, the corn bread on page 85 or the soda bread on page 86 .

SERVES 4 LOUNGING HUMANS

2 eggs

½ cup (120ml) milk *almond or coconut milk for dairy-free folk*

salt and pepper to taste

8 slices of your chosen bread *go on, use the banana one!*

butter and sunflower oil, for the pan *just oil if you're dairy free*

1   Crack the eggs into a big shallow bowl, pour in the milk, season with salt and pepper and whisk it all up.

2   Put a good non-stick pan on a medium-high heat.

3   Dip each slice of bread into the egg mix and turn to make sure the bread is coated on both sides. I like to also give the bread a little squish with my fingers so it rebounds and soaks up more egg mix – this stops the centre from being too dry. Repeat till all your bread is done. This is a great way to use up bread that might be going a little dry or hard as it will get moisture and softness from the eggs.

4   When the pan is nice and hot add a little oil and butter. The oil stops the butter burning. Swoosh the butter and oil around the pan. Sometimes I gently rub it down with a bit of kitchen towel so it's not too oily.

5   Depending on the size of the pan, I usually fry about 2 slices at a time, as adding more just lowers the heat of the pan and stops the French toast from sealing properly. Fry on both sides until golden brown. Repeat till all the slices are done. If I'm paranoid it's not cooked through, I cut one slice in half just to check.

TO SERVE

For me the classic is a side of burnt streaky bacon, while the French toast is covered in maple syrup and a squeeze of lemon juice. Also super tasty are: Greek yogurt and honey; sugar and lemon; stewed berries and honey.

Faked Baked Beans

Maybe my fascination with beans on toast is a hang-up from student days, or it could just be because it's a classic comfort food for cold winter months. After realising the amount of sugar in regular tinned baked beans I decided to have a crack at making a more exciting version for myself. These keep well in the fridge for few days and are also nice on a baked spud with a bit of grated cheese. They're named 'faked' as there is no baking involved!

1 Put the butter in a medium-sized pot on a medium-high heat. When the butter is entirely melted, pop in the onion and sauté (stir around loads) till it's translucent and a light golden colour.

2 Next chuck in the tinned tomatoes, apple of your choice and bay leaves and season with salt and pepper.

3 Let that simmer away while you open your tinned beans. Throw them into a colander and rinse under a cold tap to get that funky-looking bean juice off. Yuk. I was lazy and didn't do that once. It's gross – don't do it! Let the beans sit and drain.

4 When the tomato sauce is hot and bubbling, remove it from the heat and let it cool a bit. Remove the bay leaves – these are just for flavour and are not meant to be eaten. No Snow White moments here, please.

5 You can blend the sauce in the pot, but I transfer it to a tall, thick plastic container, as I've ruined too many white tops trying to do it the other way. Using a hand blender, blend until the sauce is lovely and smooth.

6 Lash the tomato sauce back in the pot and chuck in the tinned beans and maple syrup. Let that simmer away for up to half an hour. The beans will thicken the sauce nicely. You can taste it and season it some more if you like. Some people put a pinch of cinnamon in their baked beans, but since I put cinnamon in pretty much everything else, I don't bother here.

MAKES 4 PORTIONS

1 tbsp butter

½ small white onion, finely chopped

400g tinned chopped tomatoes

4 tbsp apple compote (page 45) or 1 sweet apple, peeled and chopped

2 bay leaves

salt and pepper, to taste

400g tinned mixed beans

400g tinned butter beans

2 tbsp maple syrup *but brown sugar would also do*

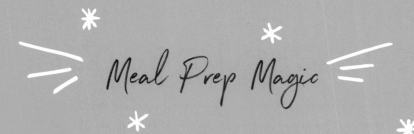

Meal Prep Magic

In a world of too little time and information overloads, here are some simple tips for healthy eating, active living and a little more time to chill.

A serious buzz phrase for bodybuilders and weightlifters is meal prep – Meal Prep Monday, Meal Prep Sunday: you get the idea. Basically you make a menu of what you would like to eat for the week and do your big shop (on Sunday for example) and then spend an hour or so prepping your meals for the week.

One of the reasons my dad thought I did well in college was due to my regular gym routine and healthy diet. It actually hadn't occurred to me, but it made sense. The gym and swimming were great physical outlets when I was studying for my final year, as they kept me from chomping at the bit when I was stuck sitting in a chair for up to seven hours a day. Eating well meant that when I had lunch and then went back to study I wasn't in a high-carb-induced coma and dying for an afternoon nap.

Now, STOP. I know you're gonna be, like, Finn, seriously, you want me to take, like, three to four hours out of my precious Sunday to shop, to cook? But, yes, that's exactly what I want. Why? Because the rest of the week you're going to have sweet eff all to think about! You've got stuff for breakfast, a bunch of things made up for lunch and then dinner is ready for you when you get home – all you need to do is heat it up. Also since I'm a coeliac – and a bottomless pit – I like to prep a bunch of snacks as well. So when 11 a.m. rolls around on a Monday morning and I'm jonesing for a sugary piece o' junk with a coffee, I have a delicious homemade (probably protein) muffin or bar to snack on instead! I get my fix and my body is the better for it.

Meal Prep Example

So in real terms what does this look like?

You should NEVER shop hungry, so on Sunday, have your breakfast – for me it's pretty much always protein pancakes, let's be honest (page 58) – have a coffee (try the Beefcake Coffee on page 316) and have a think about what you would like to eat for the week.

~~~

Here's an example of a week prepped in college. It looks a little different at the mo since I have more time:

❧ BREAKFAST ❧
Malibu Muscle Barbie Proats (page 56) *with toasted seeds and fruit or boiled egg and* **Danish Breakfast Brød** *toast* (page 34), *coffee or tea*

❧ SNACKS (MORNING/AFTERNOON) ❧
Broke-Student Breakfast Muffins (page 50), *low-fat Mini Babybels, Quest bar, bottle water, tea, coffee*

❧ LUNCH ❧
Sexy-Skin Roast Veggie Salad (page 106),
Mexican-ish Sweet Potato Pie (page 156), *an orange, a yogurt, raw veggies and mini hummus pot*

❧ DINNER ❧
Butch Burgers (page 163) *with aubergine bun and sweet potato fries,*
Siren Sea Spaghetti with Smoked Salmon (page 148)

It only took me a few minutes to think about what I would like. I've got some nice balanced meals in there, lots of protein, lots of fresh fruit and veg and healthy carbs (sweet potato and oats). It's also going to be kind to my pocket, as ingredients get used in a few bits, not like silly ingredients that you use once and then relegate to the back of the cupboard. Eggs will go in the muffins and galette and for breakfast (I usually get 12 eggs at a time), the different seeds will get toasted and go into the Danish Breakfast Brød and you can make a big fabulous salad with all the leftovers: spinach, hardboiled eggs, toasted seeds, raw veggies and a pesto dressing! Boom, a week of tasty food, a cheap budget and you can make the muffins, the pie, the pesto for the Siren Sea Spaghetti and the quinoa and roast veg for the salad on the prep day – you could prep the burgers too and freeze them (raw).

I'm the kind of person who is happy to eat the same dinners and lunches a few days in a row. If this doesn't work for you, make two variations for both lunch and dinner so you can chop and change between them. Freeze half of what you make in portions and then you have a bunch of healthy 'ready meals' stashed away for a rainy day.

Dinner

Time

The dinners I've assembled here are a rag-tag motley crew of my favourites. The order of the recipes reflects how I eat myself – a lot of inspiration from the sea, some vegetarian and meat dishes that are slow cookers, like stews and roast chicken, or a bit of charcuterie. There's a blur between dinner and lunch for me, because I often like to prep a bunch of my meals in advance. Dinner one day might be lunch the next. So here you have healthy dishes that will keep for days and can be carted around in a lunchbox, as well as fast throw-together meals.

I've chatted before about balance so in this section there's no healthy/ unhealthy division. It's all about what works for you on the day. If I've been running around like a lunatic, working, surfing and generally being hyperactive, then what better way to refuel then with the burgers and fries on page 163? Equally, if I've been slothing about watching box sets, I might just go for the fish fingers on page 139 with one of the salads from the lunch section to better suit my energy expenditure that day.

Vitamin Sea Dishes

It was with great amusement on the first day of my master's degree in Marine Biology that I discovered I was the only one in the class who ate fish. Though, to be honest, I felt a little ashamed of myself (I also used to work in an aquarium, so I felt a certain amount of guilt then too). But I believe if you're respecting the food chain and the environment as much as you possibly can, then seafood is a wonderful source of healthy fats and proteins and, in my mind, a key component of a healthy diet. When shopping for fish, get a little educated! What species are overfished and maybe should be avoided? Which are abundant and therefore good to eat? It doesn't take much time to source sustainable, good-quality fish – and your body and brain will thank you!

Garlic-Butter Breaded Mussels

I love, love, love mussels – two people's portions are more a one-person event for me. While mussels in white wine is an absolute classic, this crunchy, garlicky take on things is a brilliant crowd pleaser, easy to whip up and eaten with your hands. Tasty food, simple prep and fewer dishes to wash – what more could you want?

1 Preheat the grill to a medium–high heat.

2 Tear the bread into tiny pieces, pop into a tall container and blitz with a hand blender to make crumbs. Add the butter, garlic and parsley and mix the lot with your hands.

3 If using cooked mussels, divide the breadcrumb mixture evenly between them – I leave the side without meat on so that it can be used later as a scoopy device – then lay them out on a tray and pop under the grill.

4 If the mussels are uncooked, lash $^1/_2$ cup (120ml) white wine in a pot on a medium high heat. When it starts to simmer, pour in all your mussels, pop the lid back on and let them cook in the boozy steam for five minutes. When they're done, discard any mussels that are still closed. I won't go into the graphic details, folks, just trust me, I studied marine science. Now follow the steps for the precooked mussels.

TO SERVE

These guys are super-fast and you can keep it quick by serving them with a fresh green salad and the French dressing on page 284 or take that little bit of extra time to make the home fries on page 139 for proper moules et frites!

SERVES 2 HAPPY HUMANS
EATING WITH THEIR HANDS

2 slices slightly stale GF bread

30g butter, softened

1 clove garlic, finely chopped, or ½ tsp garlic powder

1 tsp chopped fresh parsley

450g cooked or uncooked mussels in their shells

½ cup (120 ml) white wine, if using uncooked mussels

Poseidon's Fingers

Ever since I was little, fish fingers were a go-to rainy-day no-groceries kind of comfort meal that would be served up with home fries and buttery peas. While gluten-free ones are available now, it's always fun to make your own, and you get to decide the quality of the fish for yourself.

Classic fish fingers are made with cod or pollock – known as Tom Collins in the UK because someone thought pollock sounded too much like bollocks! Generally a non-oily fish is better – I tried mackerel: it was gross.

1 Preheat the oven to 200°C.

2 Scrub your Roosters and leave the skin on – lots of nutrients in the skin, don't you know! Cut them into 1cm or less slices to get that classic circular home-fries shape. Chuck them in a big bowl, pour in your olive oil and crack in your salt. Swoosh it all around with your hand so the potato has a light coating of oil. This way you still get the crispy texture of home fries, without the artery clogging. Pop them on a baking tray and into the oven. Reduce oven heat to 180°C.

3 In the meantime, let's make some fish fingers! Cut your fish into 4cm-thick strips. When I'm 'breading', I like to put the individual ingredients out in dishes and set up a little station in this order:

- raw fish for breading
- flour seasoned with salt and pepper for dipping
- beaten egg for dipping
- oat crumbs seasoned with paprika for final dip
- plate for piling up breaded fish
- hot pan ready to go!

4 So just follow the steps above: dip the fish pieces in the flour, then egg, then crumbs – some people repeat the egg and crumbs bit, but I find one go is enough or the fish gets a bit soggy!

SERVES 2 HUNGRY HUMANS ON A RAINY DAY

Home Fries
3 large Rooster potatoes
2 tbsps olive oil
salt, to taste

Fish Fingers
250g sustainably caught white-fleshed fish *e.g. cod*
½ cup (60g) GF plain flour
lots of salt and pepper, to season
1 egg, beaten
1 cup (100g) GF oats, crumbled up with your fingers
1 tsp sweet paprika
sunflower oil, for frying
optional flavours *to add some extra kick to the oat crumbs you could add some dill, lemon zest, chilli flakes or even some seaweed flakes*

5   Have your pan on a medium to high heat. Pour in a tablespoon or so of sunflower oil. I don't cook the fish the whole way in the pan – pan time is just to seal the flavour in and get the breaded part nice and crispy. Cook each piece for about 2 minutes on either side. When all the pieces are ready, pop them on a baking tray covered in baking parchment and then into the oven.

6   Mix the home fries around while you're down there so they brown evenly.

7   The fish will only need a maximum of 10 minutes and should be done at the same time as the home fries. Use this time well, young grasshopper. I usually steam or boil up some peas, make a cup of tea and get out the ketchup for the chips and apple cider vinegar for the fish fingers!

TO SERVE

Plate it all up and tuck in! My good friends from Mayo love to have these fries with 'burger sauce' – mayo and ketchup mixed together. An insanely tasty mayo can be made with 1 tsp of the preserved lemon from page 277 mashed into 4 tbsp of mayonnaise – yummy for dipping the fish fingers or the fries into.

Pae-Eile

This is my Irish bastardised version of paella, since traditionally it's made by the man of the house (but I have boobies) and it's meant to be eaten out of a paella dish (but most folks just have a pan) and it's meant to be scooped out using bread (but I'm a coeliac). This is an unbelievably tasty dish – for the last year I've probably made it at least once a month, with a little more of the ingredients I love (tomato and wine) and a little less of the expensive bits (saffron). Generally, what I make is considered paella mixta, so it's a combination of chicken, chorizo, seafood and veg.

SERVES 4 IN BIG PORTIONS BUT CAN STRETCH TO MORE DEPENDING ON HOW MUCH CHORIZO, CHICKEN, SEAFOOD AND VEG YOU TOP IT WITH

1 ¼ cups (250g) paella rice

4 cups (1 litre) chicken stock

1 small white onion

1 ½ cups (200g or half a big ring) chorizo

1 red pepper

1 yellow pepper

big handful asparagus spears

1 cup (100g) frozen peas

1 free-range chicken breast *half the time I don't bother and just go for the seafood and chorizo, but it's good for a bit of extra protein*

3 mussels for each person

2 big prawns for each person *I like to serve them still in their shells, heads and all, for the authentic look, but if that freaks you out you can use the precooked ones*

olive oil, for frying

1 cup red wine (235ml) *no longer worth drinking: don't waste the good stuff!*

1 tbsp tomato purée

1 tbsp turmeric

½ tsp cayenne pepper

1 tbsp sweet paprika *known as pimenton: I frickin' love this stuff so I use tons*

pinch of saffron if you have it *don't worry if you don't: turmeric is known as 'the poor man's saffron'*

handful fresh coriander, chopped

1 lemon, cut into 4 wedges

1   This recipe can seem a little bitty, but after a few goes it becomes second nature. Soon you'll be showing off to guests and dancing around the kitchen while you make it. The best thing to do, and this stops me burning the rice, is prep everything in advance.

2   Measure out your rice. Have a jug ready with boiled water and your stock dissolving. Have all your spices, wine and tomato paste close to the stove ready to go.

3   Peel and chop your onion nice and fine. Peel the outer skin off the chorizo and slice it up. I cut it fairly fine so the fat and pimenton from the chorizo can flavour and colour the rice later.

4   Slice your peppers into long thin strips and cut the ends off your asparagus spears diagonally.

5   Measure out your cup of peas and set them to one side. This way they can defrost a bit before they go in.

6   Cut your chicken up into bite-sized chunks.

7   Scrub your fresh mussels clean. Discard any that don't close when tapped sharply. Confusingly, if you're using precooked mussels, discard any that are still closed.

8   You don't need to do anything with the prawns if you're cooking them whole. But you can take off the heads and shells and de-vein them if you wish.

9   *Vamos!*

10   Put a large non-stick pan on a medium-high heat. When it's nice and hot lash in about a tablespoon of olive oil. Saute the onions until they are soft, take them out and put them to one side. There will be a good bit of 'putting to one side' in this recipe, so a handy thing is to have a big plate or a chopping board nearby.

11   Lash in the chorizo. There's no need to add more oil, as the chorizo will release its own fats. Stir-fry until the oil in the pan starts to take on the red colouring of the chorizo. Take the chorizo out and pop it to one side.

12   Add a little oil to the pan if you need it. Let it heat and then chuck in the chicken. Stir-fry until it's sealed and white on all sides. You don't need to cook it through completely now, as it will be cooking with the rice later. Now – you guessed it – take the chicken out and put to one side.

13   Add a little more oil to the pan and fry the rice. You want it to get less translucent. This toasting also helps the rice keep its shape. Lash the onions and the chorizo back in the pan.

14 Next I like to pour in the red wine and cook it off. This is more Italian than Spanish and stolen from risotto recipes. I think it adds an extra depth to the paella, and it makes the rice go purple!

15 Now add the tomato paste, spices and a little of your stock if it's looking a bit dry. Allow the spices and tomato to completely coat the grains of rice. Fry for a few moments and then add the rest of the stock.

16 More confident paella makers will just lash in all the stock and let it do its own thing. I'm more of an over-protective-mother-in-the-playground kind of rice-dish maker. I like to add half the stock, watch it for a bit, then turn the heat down so it's just gently simmering. I let it absorb the juices for 15–20 minutes, adding more stock as I go when it's looking a bit dry.

17 When the rice feels a little more al dente – go on, have a nibble – I add any stock that's left and the peas. Give it a good stir, arrange the vegetables, prawns, mussels and chicken pieces on top and cover with a big lid, using the steam to cook the veggies, prawns and mussels and finish cooking the chicken. Give it about 5 minutes and then flip the prawns over. They will turn from clear with black lines to white with pink and orange when they are cooked through. Turn down the heat and simmer for up to 20 mins before serving.

TO SERVE

Arrange the meat, seafood and veggies in portions on top of the rice. Finish the dish off by scattering fresh coriander and placing a lemon wedge on each portion.

This is the best dish for big parties and dinners. I've served it for a very classy hen weekend along with a big basin of sangria (page 317) and some salsa music!

Traditionally everyone ate the paella out of the paella dish and moved their portion around with a chunk of bread in one hand. Since these days people are less inclined to share food like this, you can hand out individual warmed plates and let everyone tuck in! Goes great with a good Rioja or the Watermelon Slushie on page 318 for a tasty booze-free option.

Irish Malaysian Noodle Soup

Though my family have always been fairly multicultural in their dining tastes, this little number is inspired by one of my good friends from secondary school. Hailing from fairer climes, he spent a good few years trying to educate us Paddys in the ways of Asian cooking (I still can't handle noodles for breakfast). Many red faces, burnt mouths and desperately-sought-after pints of milk later, here is the result: a dish that can be made more or less 'Irish' according to your tastes/bravery levels where chillies are concerned. This makes a fantastic light summer dinner or, alternatively, a good lunch to set you up for the rest of the day.

SERVES 2 HUNGRY HUMANS

4 large or 6 small shallots

coconut or sesame oil, for frying

2 portions rice noodles *always check packet for GF*

handful Chinese broccoli *normal will do if you can't find it*

10 GF fish balls *not as obscene as they sound: these can be sourced from any good Asian market*

1 tsp fresh ginger, finely chopped

5 thinly sliced mushrooms *shiitake, if you're getting really authentic about it*

4 large pak choi leaves, shredded

1 tsp Chinese five-spice powder

splash GF tamari soy sauce

½ Knorr Vegetable Stock Pot or sachet (18g)

instant miso soup *because of my marine science background I just can't use fish sauces: I know too much*

2 umami eggs *hardboiled eggs that have been peeled and soaked for 6 hours in 3 tbsp tamari soy and 3 tbsp water*

fresh coriander leaves

To Serve

beansprouts

Chilli and Lime Sauce (page 285)

½ lime, cut into 2 wedges

1   To start, finely slice the shallots. I tend to do a whole bag and then keep the crisp fried shallots to top other dishes. Shallots have a more delicate flavour than normal onions, which is why I prefer them here.

2   Fry in coconut or sesame oil at a high heat, stirring all the time, until crispy. Personally I like them a bit burnt. Heap them on a kitchen towel and leave to one side. Try not to nibble on them – I always lose half of them to idle hands ...

3   Bring 4 cups (960ml) of water to the boil in a medium saucepan, then add the noodles.

4   Using a steamer or a colander and the saucepan lid, steam the broccoli above the noodles.

5   Cut the fish balls in half and then, in a pan, stir-fry the ginger, chopped fish balls, mushrooms and pak choi, seasoning them with the Chinese five-spice powder.

6   When the broccoli is done, set it aside. Then, when the noodles are al dente, drain them and then pop them back in the pot with 3 cups (720ml) of fresh boiling water. This gives the soup a less starchy base. Add a dash of tamari soy sauce and the Stock Pot or miso sachet and simmer for 3 minutes.

TO SERVE

Place the noodles and broth in large soup or ramen bowls. Arrange the stir-fry mix, broccoli and umami egg slices as you like. Garnish with lots of crispy shallots, fresh coriander, some beansprouts, a dollop of chilli sauce and a lime wedge. The chilli sauce is hot – 1 tsp for the normal, 2 for the brave, 3 for the insane. Some folks like a bit more soy sauce so leave this on the table.

For a veggie-friendly version, leave out fish balls and add another egg. For a less spicy version, leave out fresh ginger and chilli sauce.

If you don't have all these ingredients to hand, the recipe still works with the following left out: fish balls, pak choi and ginger. Carrot strips can be substituted for the broccoli.

Irish Malaysian Noodle Soup, page 144

Siren Sea Spaghetti with Smoked Salmon

Your guests will be singing your praises! This is one of my specialties – it's simple and earns you some serious foodie credit. The secret is my favourite ingredient – sea spaghetti. This stuff is the pasta bomb. Forget messing with spiralisers, this is GF, insanely low carb and, best of all, it actually has the consistency of pasta and it's packed full of vitamins, minerals and fibre. Hello, lovely skin!

For absolute knock-your-socks-off taste, use freshly made Almond Vegan Paleo Pesto (page 288); but in a pinch, a nice store-bought pesto does the job. I hate the phrase, but this is a fantastic 'free from' meal if you've any folks with a food intolerance. It's dairy and gluten free and can also be made paleo/vegan friendly if you ditch the regular pasta or salmon and just use the sea spaghetti.

I served this up to my surf girls on a recent freediving trip and they were well amused at eating what we'd been swimming in!

SERVES 5 OR 4 HUNGRY FOLK JUST OFF THE BEACH

100g sea spaghetti *health-food stores have it and if you're an experienced forager you can also get it yourself (the spring growth only needs ⅓ the cooking time)*

125g GF spaghetti *corn-based varieties hold their shape best*

salt

400g smoked salmon

½ quantity Almond Vegan Paleo Pesto (page 288) or 1 whole jar (190g) store-bought green pesto

1 This is super-fast to prep, and even quicker if you rally up a few troops to help.

2 Soak the sea spaghetti in water just off the boil for 5 mins – this gets rid of that overly seaweedy smell. Then drain, add fresh boiled water and simmer as you would regular spaghetti for 9–12 minutes until al dente.

3 To another pot of boiling water, add the regular spaghetti and a little salt. I like to keep the two spaghettis separate in case one of them takes a little longer to cook. GF pastas can vary greatly in cooking times!

4　While those lads are bubbling away, chop your smoked salmon into thin strips. I prefer to use smoked salmon instead of salmon darnes, as someone else has already done most of the slicing. And smoked salmon has more flavour, but this can mean it's fairly salty – if you're watching your salt intake, don't season with salt or use salmon darnes instead.

5　Put a big pan on a medium-high heat and add a little of the oil from the pesto (it separates a bit in the jar). When the pan is hot, lash in the salmon and the pesto. When the salmon changes from dark pink and clear to a light pink, it's cooked. It only takes 2–3 minutes!

6　Now check the spaghetti pots and, if you're happy – mine need to have a little bit of bite – put the two together in one colander and rinse under the hot tap or by pouring boiling water over it (this removes any starch). Add a wee splash of olive oil and mix around to stop them sticking together.

TO SERVE

Plate up the spaghetti mix and top with the salmon and pesto. Add a little sprig of fresh basil if you're feeling fancy. A super-quick meal that looks snazzy, is low in carbs and has lots of healthy fats and proteins. Nothing fishy about that! When I make this recipe with a store-bought pesto I add a few handfuls of baby leaf spinach with the salmon and pesto for some added greens.

Veggie Delights

Often when people have tried my food or read my blog they've asked if I'm vegetarian. I was always confused by this because, of course, I've been there all the times I've scoffed down burgers and salivated over crispy bacon. But it did make me realise that my attitude to meat (and poultry) is that a little goes a long way. With that in mind, a large portion of what I eat regularly would be classed as vegetarian food and can easily be tweaked to suit vegans too. As well as earning a few karma points by being better for the planet, this is also a step in the right direction for your health (and your grocery bill)!

Meatless Balls with Spicy Tomato Sauce

My first thought when I started catering for the culture weekends at the Gyreum Ecolodge was 'Dear God, what will I feed the vegans?' While I delight in veggie-filled dishes, I'm a complete sucker for dairy – cheeses, Greek yogurt, kefir … mmm, dairy. So I needed to come up with something that delivered the protein punch the students needed for their weekend packed full of outdoor activities.

I try to keep the vegan and veggie options themed with the main dinner. I love if people don't feel left out of the main feast – it's such a communal thing with big groups. So with Mexican-style spiciness the theme for Friday nights, I started experimenting with bean burger ideas. They also serve veggies, coeliacs, lactose-intolerant and halal people too!

SERVES 4 WITH LEFTOVERS

Sauce

1 small white onion

olive oil, for frying

pinch of both sweet and smoked paprika

400g tinned chopped tomatoes

1 tsp maple syrup

1 bay leaf

salt and pepper to taste

few dashes Tabasco sauce *if you're feeling brave*

Meatless Balls

1 red onion

handful fresh herbs *I move between coriander and parsley, depending on what is looking most alive on the window sill*

400g tinned red kidney beans

400g tinned mixed beans *or adzuki or similar*

400g tinned chickpeas

1 tbsp chia seeds

2 tsp mixed Mexican or Cajun spice *I make up my own with a combo of pimenton, smoked paprika, chilli powder, garlic powder and cayenne on days of lesser laziness*

½ tsp salt

⅔ cup (100g) milled seeds (e.g. milled linseeds), for coating the outside of the burgers

olive oil, for frying

1   I like to make the sauce first so it can mellow and cook away for extra tastiness. Ideally, I make the lot the day before it gets served up. The sauce is more flavoursome and the balls are even crispier when cooked a second time.

2   Roughly chop the onion. Put a small saucepan on a medium-high heat. When it's hot, add a little olive oil and put in a little chunk of onion. If it sizzles, lash in the rest of the onion. Sauté until the onion is soft. Add the paprika and fry a little longer, till you start to get a lovely smell!

3   Add the tinned tomatoes, maple syrup and bay leaf to the pot. Put the heat on low and simmer for up to 40 minutes then take it off the heat. I strongly dislike chunks of onion in sauce so I put it in a tall, thick plastic jar and whizz with a hand blender for a smooth consistency. (If you don't have a suitable container, take the pot off the heat, cover it with a clean tea towel and slip the immersion blender in under it to save yourself from hot splatter.) Add salt, pepper and Tabasco to taste. This sauce is unbelievably tasty for the few cheap ingredients involved.

4   To make the bean balls, finely chop the onions and fresh herbs and pop in a bowl on the side.

5   Add all the beans and chickpeas to a large colander and rinse with fresh cold water (no yucky tin-water in our dish, thank you very much). Place the beans, chickpeas, onions, chia seeds, herbs and spices in a large bowl and combine using a hand blender. Consistency is a matter of personal preference. I like to leave some larger bean-y chunks, because I think it looks rustic and cool.

6   On a chopping board, spread out the milled seed mix, like you would with flour when making bread.

7   To shape the balls, take a hefty tablespoon of bean mixture and use another spoon – or your hands – to mould a round shape. Roll it around in the seed mix until it's covered. Keep the finished balls on a plate while you work away making the rest.

8   Finally, when all the bean mix has been used up, fire up the pan to a medium-high heat and add a few tablespoons of olive oil – coconut oil is nice too but it does change the flavour a bit. Use a little linseed mix to check that it's hot and sizzling.

9   Add the balls to the pan but don't overcrowd, as you need flipping room. Cooking time will depend on the stove, but I usually check them after 2–3 minutes and then turn them over till they're evenly browned.

TO SERVE

Once the bean balls are all cooked they can be served up with a salad (see page 100 for inspiration) and topped with the sauce. Alternatively serve the sauce in a jug so people can pour their own.

TOP TIPS

These guys keep amazingly well and can easily be frozen in batches once they have cooled down. They work fantastically shaped into burgers and served with sliced tomato, onion and gherkin. If you're watching your carbs, they can be done 'bunless' with the aubergine bun on page 163.

When I'm stuck for time and haven't prepped my meals for the week, I defrost a few burgers and gluten-free wraps – I love the BeFree ones. Lay out a wrap, break the burgers in half and spread along the centre, add sliced avocado, your favourite salad leaves and a drizzle of the salad dressing on page 284 for a perfect lunchbox snack.

Mexican-ish Sweet Potato Pie

This was my go-to dish during my master's year. It made such a massive tray that I could eat it five days in a row and feed friends if we were just back from a surf trip – or in the unlikely event that we were up late studying. It's cheap, tasty and feeds the masses.

SERVES AS MANY PEOPLE AS YOU CAN FIT IN YOUR KITCHEN – ROUGHLY 5–8 PORTIONS

5 skinny sweet potatoes or 2 massive ones

400g tinned mixed beans

400g tinned kidney beans

200g bag frozen veg (e.g. carrot, broccoli and pea mix)

1 red onion

olive oil, for frying

1 pack Mexican spice mix or your own mix of 1tbsp sweet paprika (or pimenton if you have it), 1 tsp cayenne pepper, 1 tsp coriander seeds (crushed), ½ tsp garlic powder, salt and pepper *careful with the quantities or you will blow your nose clean off*

cheese of your choice to grate over the top *I like mature cheddar, or a low-fat mozzarella when I'm feeling less bold*

1. Preheat your oven to 200°C.

2. Put the sweet potatoes on a roasting tray and bung it in the oven. That's right, skin and all – don't do anything to the potatoes! Let them bake till they're soft – i.e. when you smack them with the back of a spoon they are soft and squishy, 30–40 minutes. I used to boil them, but they have a much lovelier flavour baked.

3. Drain your tins of beans and rinse them in cold water. Set aside.

4. If you're super organised, defrost your frozen veg the night before. If you're not, sacrilege here, blast them in the microwave till they defrost.

5. Finely chop your onion. Heat a frying pan on a medium-high heat. When it's hot, lash in a bit of olive oil. Test it with a little piece of onion. When it sizzles, lash in the rest of the onion. Cook the onion till soft.

6. Chuck in the spices with the onion and sauté for a few minutes. In go the defrosted veggies and stir fry for 5 or so minutes. Pop in the beans and cook for a few more minutes. Set to one side while you wait for your sweet potatoes.

7. When the sweet potatoes are soft, take them out of the oven – but keep the oven on. When they are cool enough to handle, or if you have asbestos hands like me, shake them out of their skins into a big bowl. Mash using a potato masher with a little butter, or olive oil if you're dairy free. Season to taste.

8   In a baking dish, spread out your veggie and bean mix. Then spoon the mashed sweet potato on top and smooth it over. Top with whatever obscene amount of cheese you like, or leave it out for a dairy-free option. Pop back in the oven till the cheese is melted and bubbly, 10–15 minutes.

TO SERVE

Since this is protein, carbs and fat in one place, the only addition I usually go for is a little sweet chilli sauce on the side. For a vegan option, leave out the cheese and top with a 'vegan parmesan' of 1 cup (150g) salted cashews blitzed with 1 tsp garlic powder.

TOP TIPS

If you're a student, or just generally watching your electricity bills, it's pretty smart to use your oven to do a few things at the same time. When I make this recipe I will often make something else at the same time, like the Butch Burgers on page 163, to eat that evening, and then I'll keep the Mexican-ish Sweet Potato Pie for my meals for the rest of the week.

This freezes well. I separate it into portions, so if I don't have other folk to feed those go into the freezer to be eaten at some other point when I'm too busy to get groceries!

Mexican-ish Sweet Potato Pie, page 156

One-Week Veggie Lasagne

So called because I loved to make a ginormous one, stick it in the fridge and then live off it for the rest of the week. It works well reheated (I dare say it may even be yummier this way). If you have to buy all the ingredients listed, it can be a bit detrimental to the budget, so I recommend keeping it for weeks where a bit of spoiling is deserved. Christmas-exam study week always got a lasagne in reward for hard time done in the library. For a cheaper, more saintly version, grill thin slices of aubergine and use them instead of the carb-loaded pastas.

For the tomato sauce, I use a family-sized jar of any of Lloyd Grossman's pasta sauces. I also love this with my own red-winey tomato sauce (page 280), but sometimes there are just too many things to do!

SERVES THE MASSES, OR YOURSELF FOR A WEEK

1 large courgette

2 yellow peppers

1 packet GF lasagne sheets or 3 cups GF penne (when broke) or 2 large aubergines (when ditching carbs)

2 free-range happy eggs

400g ricotta cheese

1 large bag (200g) baby leaf spinach *if you wonder why I never use regular spinach, it's because life is too short to sit around pulling the stalks off old spinach. Huh, that sounds like a Chinese proverb ...*

family-sized jar (500ml) Lloyd Grossman tomato-based sauce

2 cups (470ml) béchamel sauce (page 279)

handful cheddar, for sprinkling

1 Do some prep before the show gets on the road to prevent any mid-lasagne-panic.
   · Pop your grill on a medium-high setting.
   · Thinly slice the courgette in circles or lengthways.
   · Cut the peppers in quarters lengthways, deseed and remove white flesh.
   · Pop all the courgette and peppers on a grill tray and grill on either side for 5–10 minutes. Not only does this make them way more tasty, it also ditches some of their water so you don't end up with a soggy lasagne. Why does soggy lasagne sound like a dirty joke? Anyway ...
   · If you're doing the aubergine option, slice them nice and thin lengthways and grill with the rest of the other veg.

2 Preheat the oven to 160°C.

3 Parboil the pasta sheets or pasta in boiling salted water for 5 minutes to soften them, then keep them in a bowl of cold water to one side – this stops them sticking together.

4 Now it's time to layer up!

5 First spread the courgette slices evenly on the bottom of a large ovenproof Pyrex or ceramic dish.

6 Mix the eggs into the ricotta cheese – this adds a good protein kick to this vegetarian dish and also makes the cheese more spreadable. Smooth half the ricotta cheese mix over the courgettes. This is easiest done with the back of a tablespoon, and it's even easier if the tablespoon is hot (dip it in a cup of boiling water).

7 Cover with the first layer of lasagne sheets (or aubergine) – try not to have the sheets overlapping too much.

8 Spread the yellow peppers evenly on top of the lasagne sheets and cover with the remaining ricotta cheese and egg mixture.

9 Place the spinach on top, pour over the jar of tomato sauce and then put on the last layer of pasta and spread the béchamel on top.

10 Phew! Well done. Give yourself a pat on the back.

11 Cover the dish in tinfoil and pop in the oven for about 50 minutes.

TO SERVE

Cheese! Sorry, did I shout that? I love cheese! Sprinkle the cheese over the top and place under the grill on a high heat for a minute or two – careful, though: keep watch to make sure it doesn't burn.

Now you have a beautiful homemade dish which serves well with a big glass of milk or a nice red wine if you're with friends. It's a hearty one, though, so light desserts are recommended!

Meat Lovers' Meals

Similar to what I've said about seafood, I think a little goes a long way when it comes to meat. I may be a frugal human being, but I always buy good meat – meaning organic and, for chickens, always, always, always free range. I accept the circle of life and that something has died to feed me, but there is absolutely no excuse for that animal to have had a crappy life before it got to me. One wonderful organic pig farmer said, 'My pigs only have one bad day in their lives.' So for me, meat is a treat, it is not for every day and often there won't be tons of meat in a dish – it may just be there to impart flavour and some fat (like the chorizo in the Pae-Eile on page 141).

Butch Burgers with Cheesy Polenta Fries

So maybe you're happy with the gluten-free burger buns that you find in the shop, but personally I think they're just sugar fluff. I'd like a little more bang for my buck, nutritionally speaking. I'm also happier continually stuffing my face with veg instead of bread. Anyhow, these guys are insanely delicious, easy and gluten free, sugar free and all that wonderful stuff.

1 Have a small baking tray (around 23cm square) lined with some baking parchment and ready to go.

2 Add the polenta and water to a small pot on the stove on a medium-high heat. Stir constantly and like absolute crazy so there are no lumps. This will thicken fast to the consistency of, eh, cream cheese or thick porridge? I dunno, a thick thing anyway. Add some salt and pepper and the cheese and stir until the cheese has melted in. Pour this into the lined tin, flatten out as best you can and pop into the fridge to set. This is gonna be pretty cool, I promise!

3 Meanwhile in another part of town ... Finely dice your onion. In a big bowl, mix the minced beef, onion, shredded herbs, Cajun seasoning and pepper to taste – I don't always add salt as it is often in the seasoning already, but you can check. Then add the oats and egg – if you can't have oats, just leave out both the oats and the egg. I like them, as they give it a more classic burger texture and it feeds a few more folk with the leftovers. Mix it all up nice and good and then shape into burgers. As a general rule, for this meal try to get the size of the burgers close to the width of the aubergine so they fit nicely!

SERVES 4 HUMANS ON A SABBATICAL FROM CRAPPY BREAD

The 'Fries' because some days you just don't feel like a potato

1 cup (170g) coarse maize meal – polenta

2 cups (470ml) boiling water

½ cup (50g) grated Grana Padano or Parmesan cheese

sunflower oil for frying

The 'Burger'

½ red onion *cook off first if you prefer them softened*

500g lean organic minced beef

small handful shredded fresh mint or basil leaves *trust me, it's weird, but it's good*

2 tsp Cajun seasoning

½ cup (50g) GF oats

1 egg

salt and pepper to taste *I like lots of pepper in burgers!*

The 'Bun'

1 large aubergine

2 tbsp tamari soy sauce

½ cup (120ml) water

4   Pop some cling film over the burgers and into the fridge they go, while we get on with some other stuff (this give a chance for the flavours to settle and the oats to soak up any liquid).

5   Take out your polenta mix – it sets pretty fast – and cut into your favourite shapes. In this instance rectangles would make sense, so that they are actually 'fries', but triangles work too!

6   Preheat the oven to 160°C.

7   Put a big non-stick pan on a high heat. When it's hot, add the sunflower oil. Test a little polenta fry. If it sizzles, lash a few more in. Fry as many at a time as fit in the pan and allow space for turning them over. Have a plate ready with some kitchen paper on it to pile them up on as you go. You only need to fry them long enough to get them golden on each side. When they're all done, transfer them to an ovenproof dish, cover in tinfoil and pop in the bottom of the oven.

8   Keep that pan going, folks! Add a little more oil and fry your burgers in batches. I like burgers well done so I get them good and brown on each side. Then transfer them to another ovenproof dish and finish cooking them off in the oven.

9   Preheat the grill to high.

10 Slice the aubergine into around 1cm-thick slices. In a bowl, mix the water and tamari together. Dip all the aubergine slices in the tamari mix and lay out on the grill. Grill for roughly 5 mins either side. Check frequently in case you've a kick-ass grill that wants to singe your creation!

TO SERVE

Plate up the slices of aubergine as top and bottom buns for the burgers and pop your polenta fries on the side. They have a lot of taste themselves but you can dip them in garlic mayo, ketchup or whatever you like!

To top the burger I usually do some combo of pickles (page 274), baby leaf spinach, yellow mustard and maybe cheese. I don't bother with onion slices since there is already red onion in the burger.

If the polenta fries are too much extra to think about or you would prefer a more classic potato fry, try the Home Fries on page 139.

The Ultimate Roast Chicken Dinner

Fun fact: I was a vegetarian for all of my teenage years and it wasn't till I went GF that I started trying to incorporate meat. It was only when I started studying biology in first year in college that I even became comfortable with the idea of eating an animal. So most of the meat, chicken and fish dishes in this book are later additions to my cooking repertoire. The determination to tackle my fear of raw chicken came after my second year in college in Galway, watching my friend Jenny rustle up the tastiest of chickens for our house Christmas dinner while I was relegated to veg prep. It was time to up my game! I wanted to have a variation for this book that didn't need stuffing, was dairy free and required minimal chicken-feeling-up time, in case other folks were also recovering vegetarians.

SERVES 4 PEOPLE ON THE FIRST SITTING AND
MAKES A HOST OF OTHER TASTY THINGS
AFTERWARDS

For the Chicken

1 orange

1 red onion

1 good-sized chicken (about 1.4kg) *it's better value for money and your time to get a big one and live off the leftovers for ages than make all that effort for a tiny bird!*

olive oil for basting

1 tsp salt

For the Roast Veg

2 red onions

2 carrots

2 large Rooster potatoes

2 parsnips

1 small sweet potato

6 cloves garlic

For the Gravy

1 red onion

6 mushrooms

3 cloves roasted garlic, from the roasted veg, crushed, skins removed

fat and drippings from the chicken

1 cup (235ml) chicken stock *depends on how thin you like your gravy*

1 tbsp cornflour and a little water to make a paste *if you like thick gravy instead of runny (called a slurry by fancy folk, but that reminds me of farms)*

salt and pepper to taste

FOR THE CHICKEN

1   Preheat the oven to 220°C.

2   Slice the orange in half. Peel the outer skin off the onion and cut into quarters. Take the chicken out of its packaging, cut off the string holding it together and put it in a high-edged baking tray or roasting tin – so you don't lose any lovely gravy later. Stuff the chicken carcass – yikes, delightful word – with the orange and onion segments.

3   Rub the chicken with olive oil, or pour it over if you're kind of freaked out by raw chicken. But rubbing it will give a lovely even, crispy consistency to the skin. Lightly salt the chicken and pop it in the oven.

4   For the first 20 minutes, cook it at 220°C to crisp up the skin and seal in the juices, and then reduce the heat to 180°C for the rest of the cooking time. Baste every 20 minutes (spoon the juices from the roasting tray over the chicken). If it's a little dry, you could add a bit more olive oil but you shouldn't need to. After an hour of roasting, pierce a leg with a skewer/sharp knife – if the juices run clear the chicken is cooked. If not, give it another 20 minutes. If the juices are clear, take it out and let it rest (just leave it alone!) for 10–20 minutes before you carve it, so it gets to relax a bit in its own juices. Don't worry, it will still be hot!

5   Pour the juices from the baking tray into a jug and keep to make the gravy.

FOR THE VEG

1   These guys usually only take half the time of the chicken so you can start prepping once the bird goes in. I'm not too fussy about how roast veg look so I just do nice big chunks of everything to be drowned in gravy later.

2   Peel and quarter the onions. Scrub and chop the carrots and potatoes. Peel and chop the parsnips and sweet potato. Chuck them all on a big baking tray with the cloves of garlic still in their skins. Drizzle the lot with olive oil, season with salt and pepper, swish it all around and pop it in the oven with the chicken for 30–40 minutes. On one of your basting trips to the chicken, give the veg a little rustle so they roast evenly.

FOR THE GRAVY

1   I love, love, love homemade gravy! It's just like, oh my god, so good
    I could nearly drink the stuff. Anyway! If you're not bothered, by all
    means get the ready-made stuff, but gluten-free gravy is hard to come
    by and pricy enough when you get it.

2   Thinly slice the onion. Finely slice the mushrooms. Put a small pan on
    a medium-high heat. When it's hot, lash in a bit of olive oil and chuck in
    your onion. Sauté until soft. Then add the mushrooms and fry for a few
    minutes. Add the crushed roasted garlic.

3   Pour the chicken juice and stock into the pan. Bring to a simmer on
    a medium heat. I like a fairly thick gravy so I usually only use 1 cup of
    water. If I've put in too much, I either reduce it down by allowing it to
    simmer till it's the thickness I want or add the cornflour slurry and cook
    it off for a few minutes.

TO SERVE

In my house we set the table all nice, but then plonk the chicken, roast veg
and gravy boat down in the middle of the table with knives and carving
forks so everyone can dig in themselves and get their favourite bits! I
usually just serve water with a few slices of orange with this, since the meal
itself is very rich in flavour!

TOP TIPS

The leftover chicken can be shredded and used in the yummy sambo recipe on
page 120 or in the wrap on page 114.

NOTE ON STOCK:

While stock can also be made with a raw chicken carcass (there's that word again), it works with a cooked one too! After myself and all the scavengers have had at the chicken, I pop the carcass into a massive pot. In with it go any bits that didn't make it into the roast veg, some more chopped onions, any sad-looking carrots left in the bottom of the fridge and a few sticks of celery.

Whatever edible, herby greenery is managing not to die in my garden – usually bay leaves, thyme and rosemary – is thrown in as well. Simmer that all away for ever and ever – just kidding, about an hour or two. I like to reduce it down right to a jelly. Do this by straining the liquid into a new pot through a sieve and chucking out the chicken carcass and veg.

Then let it cool. I pop it into ice-cube trays, freeze them and use 1–3 of these little stock cubes whenever I'm making a non-vegetarian soup.

I Can't Believe It's Not Cardboard – Thick Crust Pizza

Everyone has that one dish that if someone said you couldn't eat it, you'd shoot them. For me it's pizza. I love Italian food, but mostly I love pizza. When GF pizzas started to pop up it was like the fates were taunting me. I'd eat gluten-free pizza in a restaurant and they'd cook it in the oven with regular ones and I get poisoned. Then I tried buying the extortionately priced pizza bases from supermarkets – the consistency of a stale bagel!

Then one day a friend showed me how to make pizzas on a GF tortilla wrap. Revelation! Healthy pizza! But it still wasn't that bold, thick, crunchy take-away pizza. And so I crafted and schemed: there were dry crusts; there were a few rank soggy ones. Finally the golden ticket of simple ingredients was found. Eating this can cause untold levels of glee. Crunchy crust for dipping into garlic mayo? Chewy base for tearing away with your teeth? Check and check! Below is my favourite, a simple twist on the classic Hawaiian. Serve with gluten-free beer and a smug grin.

MAKES ENOUGH FOR 4 MINI (15CM) PIZZAS

Base

1 cup (120g) GF self-raising flour, plus extra for rolling *Doves Farm Organic is tip top: great ingredients and no chemicals!*

pinch of salt

1 cup (250g) Greek yogurt

2 tbsp olive oil

Toppings

2 chestnut mushrooms

2 pineapple rings in juice *not syrup, no need for that nastaay sugar*

1 cup (225g) tomato frito *a wonderful Spanish invention where they have already added the garlic and seasoning to the tomato; if your local supermarket doesn't have it, passata with some oregano, garlic powder and salt will do*

big handful (30g grated or ½ ball sliced) mozzarella for each mini pizza

2 slices Serrano or Parma ham

1   Preheat the oven to 180°C.

2   Line 2 baking trays with baking parchment – this stops the pizzas from sticking and makes them easier to move.

3   Chuck the flour and salt in a big bowl. Make a well in the middle of the flour and pour in the yogurt and olive oil. Mix the lot together with a wooden spoon to make a sticky dough.

4   Now the fancy looking bit. Pour about $1/3$ cup of flour on a big chopping board and smooth it out a bit. For non-gluey hands, quickly dust your hands with flour. I love doing this as it reminds me of 'chalking up' for weight lifting. Time to show this dough who's boss! Working with $1/4$ of your dough at a time, grab a chunk and drop it on the floured board. Roll it around till you have a floury ball – if the dough feels too wet just add more flour. Warning: this GF version will never be as gluey as regular pizza dough and will feel softer than you'd expect, so none of that fancy swinging it around the place!

5   Next, pop a ball of dough on one side of your papered-up baking tray (you should fit two small pizzas on an average tray). Cover your rolling pin in flour to stop the dough sticking. Roll the pizza base out by moving the dough a quarter turn clockwise after each roll. This stops the dough from breaking and keeps the nice round shape. Using your hands, flatten the dough in the centre and squish the edges to create a thick-crust pizza.

6   Repeat till you have 2 mini pizzas for each tray. Pop the trays in the oven for 10 minutes to partially cook the dough.

7   For the toppings, thinly slice the mushrooms and chop the pineapple into chunks. I love Serrano ham for a little twist on the classic Hawaiian – it adds such a great flavour and you can cut thin strips using a scissors.

8   Take the pizza bases out of the oven, and now it's time to customise! Do you like loads of sauce? Not too much cheese? I like a good dollop of sauce, but plenty of space for plain crust that I can use for dippies later.

9   Spoon on your sauce, spread it out then grab a good handful of cheese and sprinkle over each pizza. Pop the bases back in the oven for 5–10 minutes to let the cheese melt. After this take them out, arrange your mushrooms, pineapple and ham and pop back in for another 10–15 minutes till the cheese is golden brown.

TO SERVE

For a healthier dinner, this pizza goes great with one of the salads from page 100 and some sweet home fries (page 139). For naughty nights, scoff two of the mini pizzas, wash down with a GF beer or a nice cider and keep your crusts for dipping in a creamy garlic mayo – 4 tbsp mayo, ½ tsp garlic powder and ½ tsp oregano.

This base works brilliantly with any combo of toppings and sauces you can dream up – think salsa instead of tomato sauce, or if cow's milk doesn't agree with you, try goat's yogurt in the base and melty goat's cheese with sundried tomatoes and artichokes as a topping.

I Can't Believ it's Not Cardboard –
Thick Crust Pizza, page 170

Chimichanga

I first came across the glorious concept of chimichangas during the international-themed week of my culinary course. I was expecting big things from the Mexican day (my favourite cuisine) and, dear lord, I was not disappointed! I've since developed my own take on the classic and I love to cook it in a slow cooker, but it's still absolutely wonderful done low and slow in an oven.

SERVES 4 HUNGRY HUMANS IN NEED OF SOME SUNSHINE

1 red onion

2 large carrots

1 packet taco seasoning or your own preparation of ½ tsp cayenne pepper, 1 tbsp sweet paprika, ½ tsp chilli flakes, ½ tsp garlic powder, ½ tsp oregano

1 tsp cinnamon or 2 cinnamon sticks (that you take out later)

olive oil for frying

400g stewing beef, cubed

3 cups (700ml) GF beef stock

2 tsp cornflour

½ rehydrated ancho chilli, chopped into small pieces

1 tbsp tomato purée

400g tinned red kidney beans

1 Preheat the oven to 200°C.

2 Chop up your onion super small. Chop up your carrots into small cubes and put them to one side.

3 Put a large frying pan on a medium-high heat. Dry fry your spices to bring them to life! When they start to get a bit fragrant, pour them onto a plate and put it to one side.

4 Keep the pan on the heat and add a tablespoon or less of olive oil. Chuck in the onion and sauté until soft. Take the onion out and pop it into the steep-sided oven dish you'll use to make the chimichanga.

5 Add the stewing beef to the pan and fry it on high for a few minutes. I brown the beef in two batches to keep the temperature of the pan nice and hot. You're just doing this to seal the outside of the meat and keep all the yummy flavour in – it will cook through properly in the oven. When all browned, transfer the beef to the casserole dish.

6 Make a paste with a little of the stock and the cornflour. Add this and the rest of the stock into the pan you used to brown the beef. This is like 'deglazing' the pan, where you get any nice beefy and oniony residue into the liquid. Then add it to the casserole dish with the ancho chilli, carrots, and tomato purée and give the mix a stir.

7   Tightly cover the casserole dish in tin foil – you want to seal it really well so you don't lose all that lovely moisture to the hot oven!.(If you are using a slow cooker, pour the mix in and set to high for 4 hours minimum.)

8   Pop the casserole dish in the oven and reduce the temperature to 180°C. Leave it in for 2 hours minimum. You can reduce the heat further or add a little more liquid if you feel it's drying out – it should have the consistency of a thick sauce, like beef bourguignon.

9   About an hour before you're ready to serve it (the longer you let it cook, the tastier the sauce and the more tender the meat), drain and rinse the tin of kidney beans and add them to the casserole dish, sealing well again.

TO SERVE

There are so many things you can do with this dish! A classic would be to serve it over rice and have a nice fresh salad on the side for a bit of greenery. But when I've had leftovers I've also used it as a filling for tacos and topped it with grated courgette, Greek yogurt (less bold than sour cream), salsa and jalapenos.

Healthy Taco Fries

I'd hate to admit to the quantity of taco fries I consumed during my undergrad years. Though I do remember one wonderful night out, one of those ones when you know you've got the right sort of friends, where myself and my friend G looked at each other in the middle of a nightclub, simultaneously said, 'I'm so hungry' and promptly left to go get taco fries. We returned 20 minutes later, with no one having noticed our absence. And, yes, we did go again later with the rest of the gang. A few summers ago, living in my awesome little surf town on the west coast, I realised it was high time to get a healthier version going – something that would fit better with the up early and surf all day vibe. So here she is revamped and rebooted, a great source of lean protein, healthy carbs and a good spicy kick!

SERVES 5 FOLK PRETENDING
THEY'RE STILL PARTY ANIMALS
OR 4 RAVENOUS PEOPLE
POST-SURF

4 large Rooster potatoes or 2 sweet potatoes, washed, skins on

olive oil, for frying and roasting

salt

1 red onion

1 large carrot

400g tinned red kidney beans

¼ tin (200g) refried beans
optional, just to give a smoother texture

500g lean organic mince

¼ packet (15g) taco seasoning or ¼ tsp cayenne pepper, 1 tbsp sweet paprika, ¼ tsp oregano, 1 tsp chilli flakes, 1 tsp garlic powder

2 tbsp tomato purée

6 tbsp free-range mayonnaise

1 tsp garlic powder

1 tsp oregano

1 big handful grated cheese
I like mature white cheddar here

1 Preheat the oven to 200°C.

2 Cut your potatoes into wedge shapes. I do this by cutting them in half lengthways and then laying the flat side down on the chopping board and cutting into it at an angle. Depending on the size, you should get 6–8 wedges per potato. Put the wedges in a big bowl, pour over about a tablespoon of olive oil, sprinkle with salt and shake 'em all around. Feel free to do a little dance at the same time. I like to listen to the *Desperado* soundtrack when I'm cooking anything even vaguely Mexican. Slide the wedges onto a tray and pop them in the oven. Reduce the heat to 180°C. While those bad boys are cooking away it's time to make the chilli!

3 Chop your onion up nice and fine. Wash and scrub your carrots and cut them up as teeny tiny as you can. We are just trying to sneak veggies and a bit of sweetness into the recipe – we don't want the carrot to be a big deal! Drain and rinse your red kidney beans and open your refried beans tin if you're using them.

4 Put a large non-stick frying pan on a medium-high heat. When it's nice and hot pour in about a tablespoon of olive oil. If you're one of those folks who has trepidations about using

olive oil, you can of course use a flavourless coconut oil instead. Pop in your onions and carrots and sauté till they are soft. Take them out and put them to one side.

5   Next add a little more oil and then the mince. Fry until it browns. If it's one of those sneaky packets where they chucked a load of water in, I pour that off – no one wants soggy chips. Add the taco seasoning or your own mix and fry for 3–4 more minutes.

6   Add your tomato purée and beans, turn the heat way down low and let it simmer.

7   Check on your wedges and give them a turn so they get golden all over.

8   Make up the garlic mayo in a little bowl by mixing the mayo, garlic powder and oregano together. You can of course use fresh crushed garlic – I just prefer the powder.

9   Take your wedges out of the oven and take the chilli off the heat.

TO SERVE

In a big bowl – go on, a big one – layer up the wedges, chilli and garlic mayo and sprinkle the grated cheese on top. When I want a little extra spice in my life I sometimes add Tabasco sauce, Frank's hot sauce or pickled jalapenos.

Healthy Taco Fries, page 176

No Carbs before Marbs – Protein Pizza

This is one of my favourite 'healthy for naughty' sneaky swaps. First introduced to me a few years ago, it is so called because many folks, when heading off on holiday to the Spanish resort town of Marbella, cut out the carbohydrates before their holidays to slim down quick and ditch some water weight. For example, 'Oh my god, babe, back away from those nachos – no carbs before Marbs!' It's now become a staple for my family and friends at large. A super-fast and simple-to-make recipe, it's low carb and can be very high protein if you're selective with your toppings!

SERVES 1 HUNGRY HUMAN

GF tortilla wrap *I use BFree*

3 tbsp salsa *I use the Tesco own brand mild one*

big handful (¼ ball) low-fat mozzarella, sliced

toppings – my personal fave combo is sliced mushroom, black olives, pineapple and Green Farm Cajun chicken

1   Preheat the grill – I put mine to max power as it's a bit rubbish; individual grills vary. Put on the ingredients in the following order: wrap on tray – salsa on wrap – cheese on salsa – toppings on cheese.

2   Pop it under the grill (not too close or the cheese cooks too fast) for 8–15 minutes, depending on the grill. I always watch it for safety. Or salivation. If you're cooking this for two, simply pop them in the oven (180°C) instead.

TO SERVE

This goes great with a little salad or a baked sweet potato if you want a more filling meal.

This works brilliantly with any other combo of toppings and sauces – think classic tomato topped with pepperoni. The outside edges that don't have sauce often burn a wee bit – you can rub them with a little more salsa or just enjoy the charcoal tastiness!

Crispy Balsamic Ribs with Honey Roast Parsnip Chips

In my mind this is a really summery recipe. The first time I ever made it was for my dad and his good friends while enjoying an August sunset and warming ourselves by a bonfire on his land in Sligo.

1   Preheat the oven to 220°C. Since it's hard to seal awkwardly shaped meat like ribs in a pan, I just turn the oven up nice and hot for the first 10 minutes of cooking time and then reduce it to cook the ribs slow and low for some fall-off-the-bone tasty meat.

2   Mix the olive oil and balsamic together to make a dressing and rub all over both sides of the ribs. Season the ribs with pepper – the meat is usually salty by itself, especially after slow cooking, so I don't bother adding any extra.

3   Lash them on a tray in the oven. After 10 minutes reduce the heat to between 180°C and 200°C. I like my ribs to be super, super crispy and for the glaze to be reduced and nice and sticky, so I keep them in the oven for at least an hour.

4   Scrub the parsnips and take off the tops and tails. I only peel them if they are particularly rough looking, otherwise why waste? Slice them in quarters lengthways to make nice big wedges and pop them into a big bowl. Drizzle with oil and honey and sprinkle over the salt. Pop them on a baking tray and into the oven with the ribs they go. They take 30–40 minutes, depending on the size of your wedges.

SERVES 2–3 HUNGRY
HUMANS

Ribs
2 tbsp olive oil

3 tbsp balsamic vinegar

1 rack of pork ribs – 10–12 bones

cracked black pepper to taste

Chips
5 large parsnips

1 tbsp olive oil

1 tbsp honey

pinch salt

TO SERVE

Pop some bowls of lemon water on the table for folks to rinse their hands and serve with a light salad. I love some garlic mayo to dip the parsnips in!

Less Boozy Beef Bourguignon

Beef bourguignon is a serious favourite in my family. So much so that when we go for lunch in Powerscourt Gardens in Wicklow, there are three generations ordering the stuff. These days when I visit the fam I'm under strict orders to whip up a batch! This version of the French classic won't break the bank, clog the arteries or knock you off your barstool. Since this is a meat-heavy dish, I like it over potatoes with some greens on the side. Bon appétit!

SERVES 4, NEVER COVERS 5 BECAUSE PEOPLE WILL LITERALLY LICK THE PLATES

500g stewing beef, cubed

olive oil for frying

2 cups (470) GF beef stock

1 bouquet garni *fancy term for aromatic herbs lashed together with a bit of string. I like a combo of fresh rosemary, thyme and 3 bay leaves – all together, it should be about a handful*

500ml cheap/leftover red wine

1 tbsp cornflour

4 large carrots

½ cup (80g) cocktail onions *often they are in vinegar and this works no problem: just avoid the ones in malt vinegar*

200g chestnut mushrooms *not in keeping with the classic, but I love their meaty texture and prefer the flavour*

16 baby potatoes – 20 if they're really tiny

pinch of salt

4 asparagus spears per person

a little butter and lemon to serve

1 Preheat the oven to 180°C – or you can cook in a slow cooker on high for 6–8 hours.

2 On the stove, put a large frying pan on a medium-high heat. When it's nice and hot add some olive oil. Fry the beef in two separate batches. This stops the pan from cooling down too much when you chuck in the beef and means the meat seals all that yummy flavour in!

3 Put the stock, beef and bouquet garni (most people tie this up with string – I'm terrified of using string in food ever since watching *Bridget Jones's Diary*) into a deep-sided casserole dish. Cover it super-duper tight with tin foil and pop it in the oven.

4 While alcohol generally burns off at just below 80°C, it can actually be a higher temperature when it's mixed with other compounds (like the food). As quite a few of my friends and family don't drink and I want to take the booze-laden feel out of this dish, I cook the booze off by itself and also use this time to thicken the sauce. (You can skip this step and add the wine into the casserole dish with the rest if you prefer.)

5 Put the frying pan back on a medium-high heat – you should still have some lovely meaty juices in there, so no point in wasting them. Pour in the wine and let it simmer away. While that's going on, I make a little paste with the cornflour and

a little water. Add this to the simmering wine. Reduce until you get a gravy-like consistency. Or until you're drunk off the fumes! Take the casserole dish out of the oven, add the wine sauce and pop the dish back in the oven.

6   Now I like to get everything else prepped and then wander off for 3 hours (or 6 if you're using the slow cooker) – still in the house, mind, for fear that I might burn it down. Chop the carrots up nice and small (think 1cm cubes), drain the vinegar off the onions and cut the mushrooms into quarters, or sixths if they're big.

7   Three hours later: add the mushrooms, carrots and onions. Put the potatoes on a baking tray, drizzle with olive oil, sprinkle with salt and lash them in the oven with the casserole. If you're using a slow cooker, simply put them in the pot.

8   Forty-five minutes later (lol, did you think this would be a quick recipe? It's French food, for goodness sake): steam the asparagus on the stove top – either in a steamer or a metal colander with a lid over it above a few centimetres of water in a pot.

TO SERVE

It's finally ready but, by Jove, it was worth the wait! Divide the potatoes between the bowls, ladle the bourguignon over and top each with some asparagus, a squeeze of lemon and a little bit of butter, et voilà!

A note on salt and slow-cooked things: I added salt to the potatoes only, as there is already salt naturally in the meat and also some in the stock. Never add salt at the start of a recipe that is going to reduce in size, as it can be way too salty by the time it finishes cooking. Over-salty food equals sad, thirsty, hungry guests.

Deep & Meaningfuls – What's Important to Me

I come from a family of well-educated, highly sarcastic, strong-headed women. That said, I have no particular motivational quotes that I live by, more just general guidelines for a good life that have been passed down to me. I've always been taught to treat people as you would like to be treated, never pretend to be stupid so that you're less intimidating, always help people with their luggage and don't be on your phone at the dinner table (ya git!).

Good ones passed down from the mammy

and the grannies include:

1

Always trade on your brains, not your gender or your looks.

2

'Be sound' – a very Irish way of saying that if you're in a situation where you could screw someone for personal gain, be sound and don't do it. An example would be not shafting someone with extra rent when playing Monopoly, also known as the Be Sound Rule.

3

Try to avoid 'bought sense' – spending a stupid amount of money on something ridiculous and only learning from it afterwards. According to my nana, this includes €2,000 loans for J1 visa trips, getting a 2-litre petrol engine for a first car and dying your hair yourself so that you have to spend 10 times that amount to get it fixed by a hairdresser.

4

Other ones include: 'An asp in the grass is a snake, a grasp in the ass is a goose;' 'You can't hold what you don't have in your hands;' and 'Wherever you be, let your wind blow free.' (It's charming to know that most of the life lessons passed by my family are about farting when you want to and not being an idiot.)

5

And last but not least, an absolute gem from Dad that has kind of become his catchphrase: 'Keep the faith in in-between times' – best served up when someone is anxiously waiting for something important, having a financial meltdown (but money is on the way) or having a dry spell in the love-life department.

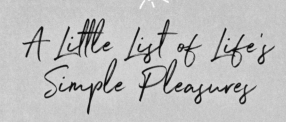

A Little List of Life's Simple Pleasures

Because why not? I like to make a list of the good little things in life when the big things in life are getting me down. My friends and family call this 'being easily amused'.

1
Snuggling up on the couch in laundry that's fresh out of the dryer

2
A good cup of tea (usually better when made by someone else and you've just come in from the cold)

3
Popping bubble wrap

4
Learning swear words in foreign languages

5
When someone else's dog gets really excited to see you

6
Freshly squeezed orange juice in the morning

7
The heatwave when you get off a plane (in a hot country)

8
Realising the new TV programme you have just become addicted to has more than three seasons

9
Advent calendars with good quality chocolate behind the number

10
The smell of freshly ground coffee

Just

Desserts

These are simple, tasty treats, so there's no compromise going gluten free, but you won't have steam coming out your ears thanks to difficult recipes or trying to source elusive ingredients.

The desserts here fall into two very different categories: from the completely naughty Bold Bread and Butter Pudding (page 225) and Banoffee Pie (page 228) to the gluten-free, dairy-free, refined-sugar-free, nut-free Everyone Ice-Cream (page 221) which is high in potassium. This is because they're divided between the dishes I was sad I couldn't have any more when I went GF, like carrot cake, and the healthier sweet treats that I actually have regularly. I'm always harping on about balance, so this is reflected in my desserts as well. Generally speaking, I eat healthy. But I don't believe in deprivation. When I travel I always want to try the local treat – gelato in Italy, custard tarts in Portugal. If I can't have it, you can sure as hell bet I'm going to try and recreate it later!

Key ingredients for a lot of the baking here are things like maple syrup and ground almonds. While these can seem like fairly pricy ingredients, if you're stocking up when you're in a big supermarket and having a muffin or a slice of something from this book instead of a store-bought gluten-free sugar-laden treat, it saves moolah in the long run and it's better for your body!

You might wonder why I don't have a chocolate cake recipe. Since I usually end up having it when I'm eating out, I don't usually bother making it for myself. Also when I have tried to devise my own recipe, it has never been as tasty as Donal Skehan's recipe or the one I used to bake in the Fumbally Café in Dublin (now go try those: they are to die for!). In the future I might have another crack at it, but until then try the Sod of Turf Brownies on page 218. They are frickin' awesome! Also you could just make that recipe in a cake tin and pretend it's a chocolate fudge cake!

Cork Winter Drizzle Blasters

These little guys were an invention to get me through the 11 a.m. drizzle of Cork City when I was studying. Thankfully these days they are more likely to be served with a bit of sand on the beaches of the north-west coast of Ireland. Originally peanut-butter muffins occasionally smothered in Nutella, the chocolatey goodness eventually made it into the recipe due to demand from the housemates! While most folks fight over whose turn it is to buy milk, our house kept up a steady Nutella addiction.

1   Preheat the oven to 180°C.

2   In a big bowl mix the flour, ground almonds and baking powder.

3   Scoop the peanut butter and Nutella into a microwavable jug and melt carefully in the microwave. I usually do this for 30 seconds at a time till it's melted and just warm – too hot and the Nutella separates.

4   In another big bowl add the eggs, oil, honey and banana. Blend with a hand blender. Stir the peanut-butter and Nutella mix into this with a big wooden spoon.

5   Slowly incorporate the dry-ingredient mix into the wet ingredients. You want a thick, chocolatey-looking batter.

6   Grease the cups of a muffin tin with some butter or coconut oil and scoop in the muffin batter. Pop in the oven and bake for 10–15 minutes until a clean knife poked in comes out with no crumbs.

MAKES 12 LITTLE MUFFINS OR 8 MASSIVE ONES

1½ cups (180g) GF self-raising flour

1 cup (120g) ground almonds

2 tsp GF baking powder

½ cup (135g) smooth peanut butter

½ cup (150g) Nutella

2 eggs

⅔ cup (160ml) coconut oil, melted, or sunflower oil

⅓ cup (80ml) honey or maple syrup *if you don't have a terribly sweet tooth you can leave this out: there's plenty of sweetness between the banana and the Nutella*

1 slightly brown banana

TO SERVE

Take them out and let them cool a little on a wire rack. Myself and the girls love these guys for a post-surf snack on the beach with a Thermos of coffee, and they are great for elevenses at work too!

Yahoo, I Can Still Have Crumble

I think crumble is a major staple when you're starting out eating gluten free. It's simple and since the main ingredients are oats and fruit, you don't even need to feel that bold having it for dessert – disclaimer: I often have the leftovers with Greek yogurt for breakfast!

SERVES 8–12

Base

5 large cooking apples or 10 eating apples *reduce the maple syrup or honey if using eaters, as they are naturally sweet*

1½ tsp ground cinnamon

250g frozen mixed forest fruits

½ cup (120ml) maple syrup or honey

Crumble Topping

2½ cups (150g) GF oats

½ cup (70g) milled seed mix

½ cup (70g) ground almonds

3 tbsp (45g) butter, taken out of the fridge for a while to soften *or coconut oil if you want a dairy-free version*

1 tsp orange zest *my aunty taught me this trick: it adds a real zing!*

1 Preheat the oven to 180°C.

2 Depending on your preference, you can peel the apples or not. I tend to only peel them if they're cooking apples. Thinly slice them.

3 Line the bottom of a casserole dish with the apples and sprinkle with cinnamon. Next layer over the berries and drizzle over the sweetness – honey or maple syrup. I lash this mix into the oven while I make up the crumble topping so that the berries can thaw out and the apples get really soft and juicy. Not doing this can mean the crumble gets a bit soggy.

4 In a big bowl mix together the oats, milled seed mix and ground almonds. Chop up the butter and work it in with your hands to make, you guessed it, crumbs! If you're using coconut oil, just melt it by popping it in a bowl and into the microwave for 30 seconds to 1 minute (depending on how cold your house/kitchen/country is). It can be hot when you take it out, so stir it in with a wooden spoon instead of your hands!

5 Take your fruit mix out of the oven and smother it in the crumble layer. Sprinkle over the orange zest. Lash it in the oven for 20–30 minutes until the crumble is golden.

TO SERVE

Hot, hot, hot with custard, ice-cream, cream, all of them, whatever brings you joy! If you're a dairy-free human, serve it with Everyone Ice-Cream (page 221) or some coconut yogurt.

Lazy Man's Pear Crumble

For those days when you suddenly want dessert, but you've no fresh fruit in the house and you really can't be arsed with that much prep, this is a ridonculously straightforward crumble.

1 Preheat the oven to 180°C.
2 Slice the pears thinly in whatever shape you like and use them to line the bottom of a casserole dish. You don't need to add any sweetness to the pears – just drain off the juice so the crumble doesn't get soggy.
3 Cover the pears with the crumble mix.
4 Bake in the oven for 20–30 minutes until the crumble is golden brown.

TO SERVE

If you want a treat, smother the crumble with custard (my favourite!), cream or ice-cream. For less naughtiness you could use natural or Greek yogurt.

SERVES 8

800g tinned pear halves in juice

crumble topping (page 196)

Elderflower and Redcurrant Muffins

These dainty little ladies came about one weekend when I wanted to make treats for guests (or maybe just myself ...) after their day of surfing and hiking. However, I didn't have any of the chocolate or maple syrup I needed to make my usual muffins. I also didn't have any sugars or honeys. Basically, I had a redcurrant bush in the garden and a bottle of elderflower cordial that had been keeping me on a constant sugar high since I'd made it. And so necessity begat deliciousness. These little fellas are perfect for a picnic on the beach or brought to impress your granny with tea.

MAKES 12 SNAZZY-LOOKING LITTLE MUFFINS OR 8 BIGGER ONES

1 large or 2 medium eggs

⅔ cup (130ml) sunflower oil, plus extra for greasing

1 banana, mashed

⅔ cup (130ml) elderflower cordial

1 cup (120g) ground almonds

1¼ cups (180g) GF self-raising flour

1 tsp GF baking powder

1 cup (125g) redcurrants

1   Preheat the oven to 180°C.

2   In a bowl, beat the egg(s), oil, banana and cordial together.

3   In another bowl, mix together the ground almonds, flour and baking powder.

4   Add the dry bowl to the wet bowl and mix until you have a lovely smooth, light-gold batter. Stir in the redcurrants. If they get beaten around a bit you get pink muffins; if you're gentle you get red polka dots. It's up to you!

5   Grease a muffin tin with a little sunflower oil – I usually use about 1 teaspoon for the whole tray and rub it into the muffin cups with a bit of paper towel.

6   Pour the batter evenly between the moulds and bake in the oven for 10–15 minutes. They're done when they are a light golden-brown colour and a knife/chopstick/whatever comes out clean when you poke it into one of the muffins.

7   Put the muffins on a wire rack to cool. Or if you can't wait that long, try not to burn your hands while you enjoy them with a mug of tea.

TOP TIP

These guys keep well for ages as they are made with almonds so don't dry up too quickly.

Protein Muffins

These were an important part of getting me through the college day. I will put my hand up and say that I have a demon of a sweet tooth. I just need, need, need something to hand at 11 a.m. with a coffee or, God help the world, I'll be eating all the sweet things I can buy! The simple answer was to bring something just a little less naughty with me. But this is also the saving grace of evening study sessions. It's more of a baked good than a dessert, but no less important!

1   Preheat the oven to 180°C.
2   Grease a muffin tin with coconut oil.
3   In a mixing bowl, add all the dry ingredients and stir 'em up.
4   In a big mixing bowl, add the wet ingredients and whizz them with a hand blender.
5   Lash the dry bowl mix into the wet bowl and stir into a batter.
6   Mix in any extras you want to add.
7   Pour into the muffin tin.
8   Pop in the oven for 10–16 minutes – depending on how big you made the muffins/brilliance of your oven.

TO SERVE

Well, that was fast, wasn't it? These are a reasonably saintly muffin, so to be bold I'll often lash them in the microwave for 30 seconds and then lather them with Nutella.

MAKES 12 LITTLE MUSCLY MUFFINS

Dry Bowl

2–3 scoops (60–90g) vanilla protein of your choice

2 cups (440g) ground almonds

2 tsp GF baking powder

2 tbsp cocoa powder

Wet Bowl

2 eggs

⅔ cup (140ml) coconut oil, melted

2 ripe bananas

⅓ cup (80ml) maple syrup
I generally leave this out if the bananas are very ripe, as there is already sweetness in the protein

Optional Extras
I like muffins to have a bit of variation in texture so will often add some of the following

¼ cup (40g) cacao nibs – for crunch

½ cup (90g) dark chocolate chips – for a treat

½ cup (60g) chopped pecans – for texture and caramely flavour

Coconut Banana Muffins with Molten Dark-Chocolate Core

These guys seem pretty naughty, what with the dark chocolate and all, but they are actually very nice! An absolute godsend for dairy-free folk (check that the dark chocolate has no dairy first), I used to love making these for my lactose-intolerant friend in Cork, as she rarely got to enjoy muffins or chocolatey treats. These muffins have a lot of healthy fats, are great for your hair (thank you, linseeds) and keep for ages!

MAKES 6 – DOUBLE THE RECIPE IF YOU WANT A LOAD, BUT THESE LADS ARE FAIRLY DECADENT

Dry Bowl

1 cup (120g) ground almonds

¼ cup (60g) ground linseeds

¼ cup (40g) desiccated coconut

pinch of salt – I like pink Himalayan

1 tsp GF baking powder

Wet Bowl

¾ cup (150g) coconut oil

2 slightly brown bananas

2 medium eggs

3 tbsp maple syrup (optional)

60g or so 70% dark chocolate
if you get a dairy-free bar then these muffins are DF as well as GF

1. Preheat the oven to 180°C.

2. In one bowl, mix all the dry ingredients.

3. In the other bowl, add all the wet ingredients. Due to Ireland's pesky climate, coconut oil is usually solid at room temperature so you may need to heat it up – either in a pot on the stove at a medium heat (usually 3–5 minutes till it's liquid) or in a mug in the microwave (a 700W microwave takes 30 seconds).

4. For pure laziness, blend the wet bowl with the hand blender. It takes 2 seconds and requires no elbow grease.

5. Pour the dry bowl into the wet bowl. (I tend to make this recipe in the morning while I'm still a pre-coffee zombie, hence the simplicity.) Mix them, MacGyver!

6. Use a little coconut oil to grease the cup-shaped bits of the muffin tin.

7. Pour the muffin mix in as evenly as you can – but I like to make a few big fat ones for those days when I just need a little thrill.

8. Now break up the chocolate into small chunks roughly the size of a grape. Push a chunk into the middle of each muffin and smooth over the top to seal the chocolate in!

9   Pop the tin in the oven. I tend to check them at around 10 minutes (out of paranoia and to turn them around) but they usually take 16–20 minutes. Your muffins are done when you poke a knife – I use a wooden chopstick instead – into one of the muffins and it comes out clean.

TO SERVE

These make the best elevenses ever with coffee or tea. If you've managed not to demolish them straight out of the oven, the chocolate can be melted anew by giving the muffin a 20ish-second blast in the microwave when you're ready to eat it.

TOP TIPS

If you want these guys to look all fancy, take them out halfway through baking and top each muffin with a walnut half and a slice of banana.

Since these muffins are high in healthy fats – thank you, coconut, linseeds and egg! – they don't dry out and are therefore a perfect travelling companion, whether you're running errands or heading to the airport.

These lads also freeze well so you can go nuts and make enormous batches.

Lemon Curd Almond Cups

These little guys look so fancy but, shhh, really they are just a great way to make a dessert for loads of people that uses just one big bowl! I do them in little ovenproof cups and make a huge lot to serve after dinner parties.

1 Preheat the oven to 160°C.
2 Mix the icing sugar and eggs together, making sure there are no lumps. Add the lemon zest and the ground almonds.
3 Melt the butter in a bowl in the microwave – I usually do 30 seconds at a time, so it's just melted. Mix the butter and lemon juice and add the egg and ground almond mix.
4 Line your serving dishes up on a baking tray – they can be ramekins or ovenproof cups: whatever you like. Divide the mix evenly between the cups.
5 Pop in the oven and bake for 15–20 minutes. The curd will have set and have a golden coating of almonds on top.

TO SERVE

When they've cooled a little bit, use a piping bag to pipe on some chilled mascarpone in the same way you would cream or icing. Top with a little biscuit – these can be used to scoop out the curd. Serve warm after dinner with tea or coffee.

MAKES 12 LITTLE CUPS FOR HAPPY, WARM TUMMIES – ALSO STRETCHES OUT WELL TO FEED THE MASSES

2 cups (400g) naughty white icing sugar

6 eggs

6 lemons, juice of all and zest of 4

1½ cups (200g) ground almonds

1 cup (220g) real butter

1 cup (200g) mascarpone cheese

6–12 thin GF biscuits, depending on size

Coconut Banana Cake

This is probably my absolute favourite cake. Then again, I'm sure I've said that to lots of other cakes at some point. While I love, love, love banana bread, I'm also coconuts about coconut and I love tropical-flavoured things. I wanted to bring the two together and what a marriage it made. This bad boy is gluten, dairy and refined-sugar free. But more importantly, it's tasty cake.

MAKES 1 THIN (BUT
DECADENT) 23CM ROUND
CAKE OR 1 PERFECTLY SIZED
1 LB LOAF CAKE

**2 cups (160g) desiccated
coconut**

**⅔ cup (160ml) coconut oil,
melted**

2 large or 3 medium eggs

**4 bananas – 2 ripe ones for the
recipe and 2 newer ones for
the top**

½ cup (130ml) maple syrup

**1 cup (120g) GF self-raising
flour**

1 cup (120g) ground almonds

2 tsp GF baking powder

1 Preheat the oven to 180°C.

2 On the stove, put a non-stick pan over a high heat. Dry fry the desiccated coconut until it turns a light golden colour. The recipe is still delicious if you don't do this, but I think it adds an extra oomph! Put the coconut to one side on a big plate and let it cool.

3 In a big mixing bowl, add the coconut oil, eggs, 2 ripe bananas and maple syrup. Blend it all with the hand blender. If you're determined to get a workout in, you can do it by hand and mash the bananas with a fork on a plate first.

4 In a smaller mixing bowl, mix the desiccated coconut, flour, ground almonds and baking powder.

5 Pour the dry mix into the wet mix bit by bit, incorporating as you go.

6 Line a 23cm round cake tin or a loaf tin with baking parchment. I use the 23cm tin if I want a decorative cake and the loaf tin if I want to pre-slice the cake and freeze it to have a slice each day with my lunch or morning coffee.

7 Pour in the cake mix. Bake in the oven for 40 minutes. Halfway through baking time, if I'm doing a round cake, I slice the two fresh bananas into super-thin slices and lay them across the top of the cake, then pop it back in the oven for the last 20–25 minutes so they dry out. You end up with a beautiful, natural-looking cake, perfect for a party.

TO SERVE

You can make this cake even more of a health superstar by lowering the sweetness count. While I love a sweet treat, it doesn't take a lot to satisfy my sweet tooth (I love dark chocolate). If I'm using super-ripe bananas I might chuck a third one into the mix and leave out the maple syrup altogether.

I tend to serve this cake by itself, as it's decadent and rich all on its own. It's a perfect pick-me-up with a nice cup of strong coffee!

Pumpkin-less Pie

Sometimes I just totally jump on the American holiday bandwagon when it comes to food. I can't help it. I blame the Internet. I'm yearning for pumpkin pie as soon as the leaves start to turn brown. Problem is, pumpkins in Ireland don't tend to show up until Hallowe'en (did you know pumpkin carving actually came from the Irish tradition of carving turnips?) and they're the decorative variety, so tend to be a bit watery and gross when you try to cook them in pie. But guess what! That other new-world staple that you can get all year round, the sweet potato, makes the most amazing of non-pumpkin pumpkin pies. Yahoo! I've made this a million different ways, and it's easily adapted to be vegan or completely sugar free, since there is a lot of natural sweetness in the sweet potatoes and the almonds, but here is my absolute favourite take on it!

MAKES ONE AMERICANA-LOVING 23CM PIE

For the Pie Crust

2 cups (240g) ground almonds

1 tsp cinnamon

1 egg *or use 1 tbsp chia seeds and 3 tbsp water for a vegan version*

⅓ cup (80ml) coconut oil, melted

1 tsp vanilla extract

1 tbsp maple syrup

For the Filling

1 massive sweet potato or 3–4 of the little skinny fellas

1 ripe mashed banana (optional) *I just like the caramely sweetness*

pumpkin spice mix – 1 tsp cinnamon, ⅓ tsp nutmeg, ½ tsp allspice, ½ tsp ground ginger

⅓ cup (80ml) maple syrup

1 Preheat the oven to 180°C.

2 Pop the sweet potatoes, whole and with their skins on, in a baking dish and into the oven. Normally sweet-potato-pie recipes will tell you to boil them down to mush, but this makes them kind of watery and doesn't unlock the sweetness that baking does.

3 In the meantime, prep your pie crust. In a big bowl mix the ground almonds and cinnamon. Make a well in the centre and mix together the eggs (or chia seeds and water), coconut oil, vanilla and maple syrup, then incorporate the ground almonds in from the edges. If the mix feels a little wet, just add more almonds.

4 This is nothing like the consistency of regular pie crust, so don't worry about treating it that way! Grease a pie dish with coconut oil – if you want to take the pie out whole so you can have it on a nice decorative plate, use a springform cake tin and line it with baking parchment.

5 Pack the crust mix evenly into the dish – this doesn't need time to relax like normal pie crust, as it won't shrink. Pop it in the oven with the sweet potatoes for 10 minutes to 'blind bake', then remove and put to one side.

6 When your sweet potatoes are super soft, take them out and peel the skin off – careful, they're hot!

7 In a bowl mix the sweet potato, mashed banana, pumpkin spice and maple syrup. The syrup might make it seem a little runny but it will dry out and set in the oven.

8 Pour the filling into the pie crust and bake in the oven for 10–15 minutes until the pie looks set (no wobble).

TO SERVE

I like a big slice of this fella cold all by itself, but it is also good served hot with ice-cream, whipped cream or Greek yogurt. It works well too as mini-pies done in muffin cases, but you'll only need half the filling recipe, as the crust takes up a lot of the space!

Brown Bread Ice-Cream

When I was little we lived for a time in the Tyrone Guthrie Centre, a residential retreat for artists. On Sundays we went to the 'big house', the stately home where artists who didn't have kids stayed, and we had the most amazing dinners. Often the only child there, I would get a mini portion of whatever the adults got. I think this was a major blessing – I was never relegated to horrible deep-fried children's food! All the wonderful ladies who cooked there were Ballymaloe trained and, as you'd expect, the food was always phenomenal. I've dreamed about recreating this ice-cream ever since that time. The dream grew ever more elusive when I found out I was coeliac. But when I finally cracked the recipe for an amazing gluten-free soda bread (page 86) I figured it was high time to revive the childhood dream. So here it is, no ice-cream machine required!

Disclaimer: This recipe is made with raw eggs. While eggs are very well-processed these days, those with compromised immune systems or women who are pregnant should use their own discretion on this one.

SERVES 6 HUMANS LOOKING FOR SOME SUNSHINE

2 cups (120g) coarse brown breadcrumbs

3 cups (700ml) double cream

7 tbsp (100ml) honey

2 eggs

1 tsp vanilla extract *1 tbsp if you're using the homemade gin bourbon vanilla extract on page 296*

1   Heat the grill to medium-high.

2   Spread the breadcrumbs out on a baking tray and toast under the grill for 3–5 minutes. I usually turn them about once. They should be slightly browned and nice and crispy. Leave them out to cool.

3   I use a 1 litre plastic container to freeze the ice-cream. No harm popping this in the freezer while you get everything else ready.

4   In a big bowl, add the cream and the honey. I use a hand whisk or the hand blender to get the mixture to a soft-whip texture – not too stiff or it can go clumpy.

5   Mix the egg yolks with the vanilla in a small jug and then fold into the cream and honey mix. Add the breadcrumbs and fold in gently.

6   Whip the egg whites till stiff and then fold them through the cream mix too.

7   Pour the mix into the cooled container and freeze for a minimum of 4 hours. This ice-cream is delightfully low maintenance, as you don't need to take it out every few hours to mix it up.

TO SERVE

This stuff is heavenly all by itself, but other options include pouring a strong shot of coffee over a scoop to make the Italian dessert affogato, or if you've made the Banoffee Pie on page 228 use some of the leftover caramel to drizzle over the ice-cream.

Cha Cha Carrot Cake with Zesty Orange Icing

Oh, carrot cake, I do love you so. It was always my favourite cake as a child, so I'm not sure what took me so long to make it for myself – probably the terrifying amount of sugar that usually goes into the icing. So here is a slightly more saintly version of the classic. I'm not saying eat the whole thing in one sitting, just that it's got a bit more of a halo than your average carrot cake, but still ticks all the boxes for flavour and texture. One very sleepy evening I forgot to add all the spices, the walnuts and half the sweetness. Guess what? It makes an amazing little bread loaf! Since more good gluten-free bread is needed in the world, have a go at it this way too.

MAKES 1LB LOAF – DOUBLE THE RECIPE FOR
A BIG 23CM ROUND CAKE

For the Cake

⅔ cup (160ml) sunflower oil

2 eggs

⅔ cup (160ml) honey

1 small ripe banana

2 ½ cups (360g) GF self-raising flour *we are gonna have a lot of raising agents in this cake, otherwise it gets really dense*

¼ cup (60g) milled linseeds

pinch of salt

¼ tsp GF baking powder

2 tsp cinnamon

⅓ tsp nutmeg

¼ tsp ginger

1 cup (60g) chopped walnuts

1 cup (100g) grated carrot

For the Icing ~ the cake is dairy free without it

2 tubs (600g) low-fat soft cream cheese or quark *quark works better as it's more solid; this stuff has a seriously high protein content, making a slice of this cake a great pick-me-up and tide-me-over snack*

⅔ cup (150g) icing sugar *this is the only real naughtiness in this recipe: if I'm treating myself I use coconut blossom sugar to feel a little less bold; honey or maple syrup would make it too runny*

zest of 2 large oranges *sometimes I use 3, as I love a super-orangey kick*

1   Preheat the oven to 200°C.

2   In a big mixing bowl, add the oil, eggs, honey and banana. Blend with a
    hand blender until smooth.

3   In a smaller bowl, add the flour, milled linseeds, salt, baking powder and
    spices and mix well.

4   Add the dry ingredients into the wet ingredients and mix. You're
    looking for the consistency of a really thick batter.

5   Chuck in the carrot and chopped walnuts and give it a good stir.

6   Line your loaf or cake tin with baking parchment and pour in the batter.
    Pop it in the oven and bake for 20 minutes. Reduce heat to 180°C and
    bake for a further 10 minutes. It's done when it is golden brown on
    top and a fork/chopstick poked in comes out clean or with just a few
    crumbs, not batter. Take the cake out of the tin and let it cool on a
    wire rack.

7   In the meantime, make the icing. In a big bowl, chuck in the cream
    cheese or quark and sugar, grate in the zest. Mix it all with a big spoon or
    whizz it with a hand blender for speed/smoothness!

TO SERVE

Wait until the cake is fully cooled before you put on the icing, or the icing
will go melty and weird! Spread the icing over the top using a palette
knife, if you have one, or just a big dessert spoon. If you want to make it
really pretty, you could sprinkle pomegranate jewels, goji berries or dried
cranberries on top for a nice pop of colour – we eat with our eyes, people!

Lime Cheesecake Cups

I've served this to friends and fam and it's now a staple for catering for large groups too. It took me a long time to make cheesecake, since back in the day store-bought gluten-free biscuits were as hard as the hob of hell – as my granny would say. But from making lots of almond milk, I've been inundated with ground almonds that are kind of soggy. Lovely. Which begged the question: could they be toasted like this? What would I do with the toasted almondy bits? Lightbulb! Cheesecake base. This recipe is awesome for students, since it doesn't rely on a dodgy oven and all the ingredients can be picked up at a supermarket. While you could do this recipe in a regular 23cm pie tin, I always divide it up between little glasses and top them with piped mascarpone for a super-fancy finish – perfect for serving to guests. These keep brilliantly in the fridge. Dessert done and dusted the day before a party? Winner!

MAKES 10ISH INDIVIDUAL CHEESECAKES

For the Topping

600g low- or lowest-fat Philadelphia cream cheese *i.e. damage control*

½ cup (110g) honey

2 large or 3 small limes

¼ tsp green food colouring (optional)

For the Base

2 cups toasted (120g) ground almonds or 2 cups (150–200g) gluten-free biscuits of your choice *I use the plain digestives from Aldi, as they have a good crunch; SuperValu own-brand ones are also good*

½ cup (100g) coconut oil or butter

⅓ cup (110g) honey to sweeten, if using toasted almonds *not necessary if using biscuits*

1   In a large bowl, scoop in the Philadelphia and lash in the honey.

2   Use the finest section of a grater to grate the zest off the limes (look for unwaxed ones) onto a plate. If you have a zester, you fancy thing you, use this instead to minimise the chances of grating off your finger. Pop the zest in on top of the cheese and honey.

3   Now juice your baldy-looking limes and add this to the mix.

4   Put in the food colouring if you're using it. Blend it all up with a hand blender and taste test – add more honey or lime as you like. The mix may seem a bit runny at this point but don't worry: it will firm up in the fridge later!

5   If you're using ground almonds for the base, put a big non-stick pan over a medium heat and throw the almonds in. I'm a terrible person for wandering away from pans on the stove. *Don't* do this – if they burn your kitchen will stink! Stir them around till they go from beige to a pale brown. They will also start to smell quite lovely. Now chuck them in a bowl and add the coconut oil or butter, whichever you're using. Butter is more traditional but coconut oil makes it feel a bit more tropical! Rub it in with your hands, then add the honey and mix it all together.

6   If you're using biscuits for the base, take them out of their packet, put them in a Ziploc bag (push the air out before you close it so it doesn't just pop!) and bash the bejaysus out of them with a rolling pin. You can decide how fine you like your crumbs – I tend to bash mine to smithereens and consider it a workout. Put them in a bowl with the butter or coconut oil and mix.

7   Press your chosen base mix into your pie dish or divide it between the glasses and press down. I tend to bend a teaspoon 90 degrees and use this to pat down the mix. Please excuse my abuse of cutlery.

8   Spoon on the lime cheesecake topping and pop the lot in the fridge for at least an hour.

TO SERVE

If you're serving it for a party, take the cheesecake out of the fridge after an hour and, using a piping bag – I have a wee one from the €2 shop – pipe on some chilled mascarpone in the same way you would cream or icing. I much prefer it to either, as it has a better texture than cream and stays perfectly set in the fridge if you make the dessert the night before, and it doesn't have the sickly sweetness of icing so it won't overpower the cheesecake. Before bringing to the guests, put a little something on top, e.g. physalis or a thin bit of biscuit.

Sod of Turf Brownies

Now I must admit, apologies to any American friends, that generally I find brownies completely underwhelming. They are either too big and dry or too small and dense. Also, they are often the only gluten-free option in most places, so I feel like a bit of an authority on this. But I was determined to like them. So, in a bit of a break from the norm, these guys are dark, intense and just a little bit luxurious. So named because that is exactly what they look like!

MAKES ABOUT 12 FINGER-LICKINGLY GOOD BROWNIES

2 cups (440g) ground almonds

2 tsp GF baking powder

½ cup (100ml) coconut oil

200g 75% dark chocolate *if you use a dairy-free one, this recipe is DF as well as GF*

½ cup (110ml) coconut milk *just take the solid bit at the top, not the watery stuff*

2 tsp good quality instant coffee or 2 shots of very strong espresso

2 eggs

⅔ cup (140ml) maple syrup

1 cup (120g) smashed macadamia nuts

1 Preheat the oven to 180°C.

2 In a big bowl, mix the ground almonds and baking powder.

3 Break the dark chocolate up into small pieces.

4 On the stove over a low heat gently melt the coconut oil and dark chocolate, stirring continuously. When they have melted, add the coconut milk and coffee and take off the heat. You want it melted but not hot!

5 Add the eggs and maple syrup to the chocolate and coconut mix and beat until it's fully incorporated. Make a well in the centre of the ground almonds, pour in the wet ingredients and mix.

6 When you have a lovely runny batter, add the smashed macadamia nuts.

7 Line a square baking tin (or a casserole dish) with baking parchment and pour in the batter.

8 Bake for 30–40 minutes.

TO SERVE

These fellas are lovely on their own with a glass of milk. But it's also nice to dial down the intensity of the coffee and dark-chocolate mix, so you could top an individual brownie with vanilla Greek yogurt, ice-cream or coconut yogurt for a dairy-free option.

Everyone Ice-Cream

I know that not being able to have dessert is not the end of the world, but it's been many years now of going without at lovely dinner parties. I wanted to make a sweet treat that could suit literally everyone! This little trifecta of ice-creams was devised with my friend Momoko, whose severe skin condition makes her very sensitive to certain foods. While she was helping me with a catering project, we decided to make these little ice-cream glasses in bulk and freeze them, as a special treat for those usually left out of the sweet treats. They are gluten free, dairy free, nut free, paleo, vegan, halal, kosher and refined-sugar free! The only folk they might not suit are diabetics and those with banana allergies (of whom so far I have actually found two).

1   Peel all the bananas and chuck them into a big bowl. Blend with the hand blender until you have a smooth, creamy texture. Separate the banana mix into 3 different little plastic containers or bowls.

2   In the first bowl, add the cacao powder and mix.

3   In the second bowl, add the matcha powder and mix

4   In the third bowl, add the vanilla and mix.

5   If you are adding sweetness, mix a tablespoon of maple syrup into each bowl.

6   At this point you can either stick lids on the plastic containers and pop them in the freezer, or you can layer up your different flavoured mixes into nice glasses for serving, cling film the top and then pop them in the freezer.

SERVES 2 HAPPY HUMANS WHO'VE WAITED A LONG TIME FOR DESSERT

6 large bananas or 9 smaller ones

1 tsp cocoa or cacao powder

2 tsp matcha green tea powder *one of the only super-expensive ingredients I'll invest in; sometimes Santa puts it in my Christmas stocking*

¼ tsp vanilla pod seeds *just scrape them out with a teaspoon*

3 tbsp maple syrup *if your people are OK with a bit of natural sugar!*

TO SERVE

If I'm going the decorative route, I take the layered-up glasses out about 15 minutes before serving and give them a little dust of cocoa powder on top. If I'm doing a bowl with three scoops of ice-cream, sometimes I'll take the containers out 15 minutes before serving and give each one a little blast with the hand blender again, for a more 'soft scoop' consistency, before putting it in the bowl.

Raspberry Upside-Down Cake

This fella came around as I was doing up cake displays and realised a little colour was needed. This is an absolutely amazing recipe for a party cake, as it looks absolutely awesome. It also happens to be gluten free and dairy free. But sure who cares? It tastes good!

MAKES 1 LARGE 23CM CAKE

Dry Mix

4 cups (480g) ground almonds

2½ tsp GF baking powder

½ tsp ground nutmeg

pinch of salt

Wet Mix

1 cup (235ml) sunflower oil

3 eggs

1 cup (235ml) honey

1 orange, zest only

For the Fruity Bit

4 cups frozen raspberries (520g) *or a mix with blackberries*

½ cup (110ml) honey

1   I really like when the raspberries hold their shape in this recipe, so I'm really careful when I defrost them. You don't want to throw frozen raspberries into the mix or the batter around them won't bake right!

2   Preheat your oven to 180°C.

3   Get a pot, pour in a few inches of boiling water, pop it on the hob over a medium-high heat and cover with a large metal sieve. Pop your frozen raspberries into the sieve. The steam from the water will defrost them gently and the raspberry juice that ends up in the water can be simmered down with honey later to make a fruit syrup.

4   While those lads are defrosting, let's make the cake mix!

5   Add all the dry ingredients to a bowl and mix.

6   Add all the wet ingredients to a big bowl and whisk thoroughly.

7   Add the dry to the wet and mix until you have a thick but runny batter.

8   Line a 23cm springform cake tin with baking parchment. Make sure you cover the bottom and the sides – we want all our lovely cake to stay inside the tin!

9   When your raspberries are defrosted, scoop 3 cups (400g) of them into the base of the baking tin and drizzle the honey over. Put the last of the berries into the cake batter and give it one gentle swirl through. This gives the cake an amazing marbled colour.

10 Pour the batter on top of the berries in the tin and pop into the oven for
40 minutes to 1 hour – baking time depends on the liquid in the berries
and the type of oven. It's ready when a knife poked in comes out with
crumbs instead of batter.

11 Take the cake out of the oven and let it cool in the tin.

TO SERVE

To get the cake out of the tin and onto a plate, release the springform sides
and remove. Place a plate over the top of the cake. Hold on to the plate and
the cake tin base and gently turn it over. The cake is now on the plate and
you can carefully peel off the baking parchment. This is a really moist cake
so it keeps well for quite a few days in the fridge.

Bold Bread and Butter Pudding with Marmalade Glaze

Bread and butter pudding was actually never a staple in my family, so it found me rather late in life (kind of like cycling) when I had already been diagnosed. I've never seen it done gluten-free anywhere. So I implore you, beg you, command you to try this recipe! It is so damn tasty that it's been known to cause obscene noises while you eat it. Totally bold, this one is an occasional treat – certainly not a weekly staple.

1   A few hours before you plan to bake, cut the crusts off your bread slices and lay them out on a plate to dry out a bit.

2   When you're ready to get cracking, preheat the oven to 180°C.

3   In a jug, whisk the milk, cream, eggs, honey and vanilla extract together to make a custard.

4   Butter all the bread on both sides. Cut the square slices into triangles.

5   In a casserole dish/high-edged baking tray, neatly arrange one layer of bread, sprinkle with the currants and pour over half of the custard. Add another layer of bread and the rest of the custard. Don't put currants on the top, as they burn easily and get a bitter taste.

6   Wrap the dish tightly in tin foil and pop in the oven for 20 minutes.

SERVES 6 PLEASURE-SEEKING POST-DINNER HUMANS

1 small loaf (400g) white GF sliced-pan-style bread *a little stale is good: keep the heels and crusts to make croutons (page 267)*

⅔ cup (160ml) whole milk

⅓ cup (80ml) double cream

2 eggs

2 tbsp honey

1 tsp vanilla extract *to make your own see page 296*

butter, for spreading *use the real stuff, for goodness sake, and let it sit out to soften before you use it*

⅓ cup (50g) Greek currants *they add more sharpness than raisins*

2 tbsp of your favourite marmalade

7   In a jug, make a glaze by mixing the marmalade with 2 tablespoons of
    water – it should be the consistency of runny honey.
8   After 20 minutes, take the pudding out and spread the glaze over it
    using a tablespoon. Pop it back in the oven, uncovered, and crank the
    heat up to 200°C for the last 10 minutes. This gives a delicious crunchy,
    fruity top to the pudding.

TO SERVE
Serve immediately after taking out of the oven – the glaze should be shiny
but not runny.

Topped with custard, this dessert is pure comfort in a bowl. At the lodge
we serve this to the student groups after they've been surfing and hiking
all day!

Toasted Coconut Banoffee Pie

I realised recently that it had been 10 years since I'd last had banoffee pie. What the hell, people? That is not OK! While there are much more pressing matters in the world, and I'm sure my waistline appreciated the sabbatical, it was time to solve this problem. This recipe is sweet, sweet, sweet and certainly the naughtiest thing in here – to be saved for special occasions, marathon study sessions or any time when it is socially acceptable for you to be bouncing off the walls on a sugar buzz.

SERVES 8 FOLK LOOKING FOR SOME GOOD OLD-FASHIONED PIE

160g GF digestive biscuits *that's a regular pack minus the few you eat when you open it*

3 tbsp desiccated coconut, plus extra to decorate

2 tbsp coconut oil, melted

2 bananas

⅔ cup (150ml) whipping cream *be warned: I like very little cream; double this quantity for full pie coverage*

1 cup (200g) caramel *I use the one in the tin that the nice folks in the condensed-milk company have already gone to the effort of making*

1 No baking required here, folks!

2 Pop your biscuits into a big clean plastic bag and bash/roll them into crumbs using a rolling pin.

3 I think toasted coconut has to be one of my absolute favourite flavours and it makes something that appears kind of plain – desiccated coconut – into something spectacular. Kind of like one of those transformation rom-com movies. To toast the coconut, put a dry pan on a medium-high heat. Wait for it to get nice and hot, then throw in your coconut. Stir it around continuously so it gets evenly toasted – a nice light-brown colour is perfect. I do big batches and keep the leftovers to put on porridge.

4 In a bowl, mix the biscuit crumbs with 3tbsp desiccated coconut and coconut oil.

5 If I'm making the pie for a party, I'll make little individual portions in small glasses. If it's just to have in the house as a treat with tea, I'll make it in one big pie dish.

6 Pour the biscuit mix evenly into either a 23cm pie dish or glasses. Press the mix down with your hands or the back of a spoon (wet with a little water to stop the crumbs sticking to it). Put the pie dish in the fridge for the base to set.

7   Cut the bananas into thin slices and whip the cream. I only cover about
    half the pie with cream, using desiccated coconut to cover the rest. Feel
    free to double the cream quantity for a more traditional look. I use a
    hand blender on a low setting to whip up the cream. It should only take
    a few seconds, as you don't want to whip it too long and start making
    butter!

8   Take the base out and spread the caramel evenly over the top. I leave
    a little space around the rim of the pie in case it gets warm and the
    caramel spreads a little.

9   Layer up the banana slices over the caramel.

10 I use a piping bag to make patterns on top of the banana slices with
    the cream and then fill in the rest with a sprinkling of the remaining
    toasted coconut.

TO SERVE

Looks good dusted with a bit of cocoa powder too and is great served with
strong coffee to contrast the super-sweetness of the banoffee.

Calami-tea — Chilled-out Entertaining without the Meltdown

I used to be way too shy to invite people around for parties
– the pressure! Awkward silences ... burnt food ... so many
potential disasters. I nearly cancelled my twenty-first birthday.
So here are my top five ways to avoid a meal-time meltdown.

1

Playlist

A solid three hours of songs that won't make you cringe, easy as pie. I go for anything blues or Americana on Spotify, chilled but upbeat, and you don't need to play DJ. Good music means lulls in conversation are comfortable, not painful.

2

Simple drinks

No fancy cocktails that stress you out. Calimocho (equal parts red wine and Coca-Cola with lots of ice and a slice of lime) is simple and always makes people want to dance (probably all the sugar). Lash it into clean label-free jars if you don't have enough glasses.

3

One-dish wonders

For example Pae-Eile on page 141 or the chimichangas on page 174. That's just one big pot for you to clean the next day, along with the plates.

4

Cold starters and desserts

So you can prep them in advance and then spend time with your friends and not just in the kitchen.

5

Lights!

Nothing kills a buzz faster than a fluorescent light. I had a housemate in college (an awesome dude) who spent an hour when we moved in 'sorting the lighting' so our house had a nice chilled evening vibe. Think lamps, battery-pack strings of white lights and lots of tea lights!

Cooking, Baking and Farming Playlists

For me, cooking is active and exciting so there is a lot of classic rock. But baking is something I either do early in the morning or late at night so a more relaxed vibe is in order. I was shipped off to rural Canada for the summer of my 16th year and so began my 10-year (so far) love affair with country music. The farming playlist has some of my absolute favourite songs, frequently inflicted on the lovely Fiona of Whitehill Eco Farm as we worked in the polytunnels.

☆ COOKING ☆

Bruce Springsteen – 'Spirit in the Night', 'Hungry Heart'

AC/DC – 'Back in Black'

Hot 8 Brass Band – 'Sexual Healing'

INXS – 'Mystify'

Grateful Dead – 'Casey Jones', 'Friend of the Devil'

Rolling Stones – 'Dead Flowers'

Jethro Tull – 'Songs from the Wood'

Shakey Graves – 'Tomorrow'

My Morning Jacket – 'Tyrone'

❀ BAKING ❀

Leonard Cohen – 'In My Secret Life', 'Everybody Knows'

Blue Swede – 'Hooked on a Feeling'

City and Colour – 'Coming Home'

Norman Greenbaum – 'Spirit in the Sky'

Jack Johnson – 'I Got You'

Cat Stevens – 'Moonshadow', 'My Lady d'Arbanville'

Stan Rogers – 'The Idiot', 'Night Guard'

☁ FARMING ☁

Brad Paisley – 'Ticks', 'Mud on the Tires'

Big & Rich – 'Save a Horse (Ride a Cowboy)'

Gretchen Wilson – 'Redneck Woman'

Keith Urban – 'Somebody Like You'

Miranda Lambert – 'Baggage Claim'

Dolly Parton – 'Jolene'

Pistol Annies – 'Boys from the South'

Thomas Rhett – 'Die a Happy Man'

Entertaining & Travelling

Gluten Free

People don't talk about it enough, but when you're trying to eat healthy or you're trying to go gluten free, it's not the weekday meals that set you back. It's weekends, meals out, travelling and wanting to eat with other people that get you. In my mind there are two barriers. You're afraid you'll eat unhealthy shite that's bad for you or, and this is my biggest fear, you'll be somewhere you can't get gluten-free food, but have zero to eat or don't want to be an awkward git for the other folks you're with.

But one of the greatest human joys is sharing tasty food with the people you care about. So the easiest place to start is at home. Have dinner parties for your good friends – don't bother making a big deal over the gluten free. Gluten-free mass-produced items were so yucky for so long that people associate those words with dry, tasteless, overpriced food. So just serve delicious, nourishing food. That just so happens to be gluten free. For yourself, this means no fear of slip-ups and also the lovely feeling that you're getting to have the same thing as everyone else!

Picnics are also a big deal for my family – on the beach, on holidays, in the boot of the car in Irish summers ... So I've put together some picnic ideas as well. Finally, the barbecue – home of burger buns and barley malt sauces. Fear not. That will be tackled too!

Barbecue Menu

I think the best thing about barbecues is that you have lots of bits to pick and choose from so everybody gets their favourite.

✳ ON THE GRILL ✳

Hamburgers (page 163)
Sauerkraut (page 270)
Clonakilty GF sausages
Prawn and fruit kabobs ~ *layer up*
large prawns, a pineapple chunk,
a cherry tomato and repeat
Grilled veggies ~ *big slices of aubergine*
and courgette, corn on the cob

✳ IN THE COALS ✳

(These guys just need to be chucked in the coals as you're barbecuing everything else – you know they're done if they are squishy when you poke them.)

Stuffed Romero peppers with feta cheese,
tightly wrapped in tin foil
Sweet potatoes, skin still on, tightly wrapped in tin foil
(these will take the longest)
Large Portobello mushrooms with a drizzle of olive oil, some fresh
crushed garlic, salt and pepper to taste and fresh chopped parsley,
tightly wrapped in tin foil
Brie or Camembert wrapped in foil and stuffed
with fresh rosemary

SIDES

Sunny Summer Quinoa Salad
(page 103)
Sexy-Skin Roast Veggie Salad
(page 106)
Boiled baby potatoes *with a drizzle of olive oil
and a sprinkle of fresh parsley and salt*

DESSERTS

Marshmallows *on sticks*
Dark-chocolate-and-chilli-stuffed bananas ~ *slice bananas
lengthways (don't peel), slip in little broken pieces of dark dairy-free
chocolate and sprinkle with a tiny bit of chilli powder. Seal tightly
with tin foil and pop in the coals. The banana goes all caramely and
delicious, the chocolate melts and the chilli gives it a nice kick! If you
pick good dark chocolate this dessert is gluten and dairy free as well as
vegan and paleo friendly*
Pumpkin-less Pie *(page 208)*

DRINKS

Watermelon Slushie (page 318)
Gluten-free beers ~ *to make lemon beer, which I missed for
such a long time, add a tablespoon or so of lemon cordial to each
glass/pint of beer*
Calimocho *(page 231). Use diet cola for less of a
bangin' sugar headache the next day!*

Picnic

For me, picnics are always a little continental, probably due to a wonderful memory of picnicking near Monet's Garden in Giverny, near Paris. Think lots of rich cheeses, good quality cold cuts of meat, tasty crackers and a sharp drink.

✳ FOOD ESSENTIALS ✳

*Cold tortilla, jamon, chorizo, Serrano ham, olives,
a selection of cheeses – my favourites are Brie, Camembert,
blue cheese and Manchego*
*If you're feeling particularly industrious, the **Danish Breakfast Brød** on
page 34 can be turned into toast-style crackers by cutting oh-so-thinly and
toasting in the oven until they reach your required level of crispiness*
***Tortilla chips** with dips – **white bean dip** (page 281), **guac** (page 290) and
salsa (page 289)*

✳ DESSERTS ✳

Sod of Turf Brownies (page 218)
Carrot Cake (page 213)

✳ DRINKS ✳

***Sparkling water** and elderflower cordial
(use the rest for the muffins on page 200)*
Cava
***Coffee** in a Thermos and milk in a glass jar
to go with the brownies*

Dinner Parties

AUTUMN/WINTER DINNER PARTY

✳ STARTER ✳

**This can be gluten, dairy, nut and refined-sugar free,
vegan and paleo.**

*You just want something very light here, as both the main and the dessert are very
rich. Small bowls of the **Lean & Green Courgette Soup** (page 90) would be perfect,
as the gentle flavour won't clash with the more intense ones in the main*

✳ MAIN ✳

**This can be gluten and dairy free,
with a vegan option.**

*__Ultimate Roast Chicken Dinner__ (page 166)
For a vegan option, try **Meatless Balls with Spicy Tomato Sauce** (page 151) –
which also goes well with the roast veggies from the chicken (page 166)*

✳ DESSERT ✳

**Can be gluten free, with a dairy-free
and vegan option.**

*__Bold Bread and Butter Pudding__ (page 225)
For a dairy-free and vegan option, make a **crumble** (pages 196 and 199) with
coconut oil instead of butter and serve with coconut yogurt instead of custard*

✳ DRINKS ✳

*Water with lime, mint and cucumber
A nice strong red wine, e.g. Rioja*

SPRING/SUMMER

STARTER
**This can be gluten, dairy, refined-sugar and nut free,
paleo and with a vegan option.**

Jamon y melon – good quality cured jamon over slices of honeydew melon:
super-fast to prep and can be done just before serving
Vegan version takes just a little longer. Cut an aubergine lengthways in very thin
strips, then cut those strips in half lengthways (we are imitating the jamon-strip sizes
here). Preheat your grill to a high heat. Dip the aubergine strips in a bowl with an
equal mix of tamari soy sauce and water. Lay them out on a grill tray and grill until
soft and the edges crispy. Allow these to cool and then use in the same way as the
jamon over slices of honeydew melon.

MAIN
**This can be gluten, dairy and refined-sugar free and can be
made vegan by taking out meat, adding more veg and using
veggie stock.**

Pae-Eile (page 141)

DESSERT
**These are gluten free, with a dairy-free
and vegan option.**

Lime Cheesecake Cups (page 215)
For a vegan option, try *Everyone Ice-Cream* (page 221)

DRINKS
Sparkling water with mint, lime and cucumber
Sangria (page 317)

Gluten-Free Travel Tips

I was a pretty lucky kid – because both my parents' jobs called for a lot of travel, I was trundled around all over the world since I was a tiny tot. I travelled far more with them before the age of ten than I managed solo in my early twenties. Since we were often travelling to fairly random and remote sorts of places, the importance of car snacks and knowing how to throw a decent picnic together was instilled early.

My first few years post-diagnosis I was pretty bad at this and was often left eating junk when I was on the move. It wasn't until I really got into fitness and healthy eating that I took what I ate on the hop more seriously.

When I was in my final year in college I had a college bag, a gym bag and a food bag that I carted around with me each day. While this might sound like a bit much, think of it this way. Since I made my food every Sunday, I had most of the work done for the week and I saved loads of moolah. Which meant I managed to travel a fair bit for a student.

These are some of my go-to snacks to pick up before a journey, as well as some tips for what to go for when you're completely stuck somewhere like an airport with no ability to go outside and look for better shops.

TUPPERWARE JOCK MEALS

This is a lunchbox filled with $^1/_3$ carbs (e.g. brown rice or sweet potato), $^1/_3$ veggies (e.g. broccoli or mangetout) and $^1/_3$ protein (e.g. stir-fried chicken, turkey or lean beef). Good for trains and buses, but you probably won't get away with them on planes.

PROTEIN BARS

Portable and so handy in a fix, good for any type of transport. When I work away at sea, I bring enough Quest bars to have one a day. When I was setting out this seemed a little excessive, but it's great when everyone else is having their tea and biscuit break – you don't feel left out. I also used to trade protein bars with the sailors so I could use some of the personalised gym equipment they'd made on the ship.

BEEF JERKY

For the cowboys and cowgirls out there. I love to keep a few packs of this in my car and always for planes. As altitude changes, your ability to taste lessens, so a strong-flavoured salty snack is great – that's why people like tomato juice on planes when they don't normally have it. It's a cool sciencey thing – look it up! I find when I'm flying I crave savoury more than sweet so I take biltong, as it's called in South Africa, which is basically just dried beef with flavouring. It packs a serious protein load per gram so it's really good for helping to keep you full while you're on the hop.

TRAIL MIX

I'm always kind of wary of the ones in shops, not too sure why, but mostly I don't like Brazil nuts all that much. I like to make up my own, which is a rough mix of sunflower seeds, pumpkin seeds, raisins and dried banana chips. Don't be the jackass who brings peanuts on the plane, please. There are folks out there with seriously scary allergies!

DRIED APPLE RINGS

These things don't get much press, really, but they are pretty cheap and you can find them in health-food stores and supermarkets. They are a handy little sweet treat and, thanks to the fibre, keep you fairly full. As they are dried, they're good for the long haul and easier than bringing fresh fruit if your bags are likely to get banged about along the way.

A sample of a big food bag that I brought

with me to sail last year was:

1

24 Quest protein bars

2

Several packs of beef jerky
I would have brought more but
it's fairly pricey

3

Packets of instant miso soup
A great thing to have in your
wallet/pocket/backpack when
you're travelling, these little guys
usually have some seaweed and
tofu in them too and make normal
dried soups taste like sawdust in
comparison

4

**A big bag of fizzy jellies/
some chocolate bars that are
okay for coeliacs**
In case the plane/ canteens etc.
only have biscuits or chocolate
that's not GF. When I asked my
thesis supervisor what to pack for
my first sailing expedition he told
me, 'Bring the jellies – everyone
likes the person who brings the
jellies'

5

A 500g bag of GF oats (more
if it's for more than three weeks)
and a small tub of GF vanilla-
flavoured whey protein powder

My Ride-or-Die Products

COCONUT OIL

I have my friend little G to thank for this one. Nearly every month she'd call me with a new miracle product (silver in water, apple cider vinegar ...) but this one has been a mainstay now for nearly five years! I use it for:

♥ *Frying* ♥
*it has a higher smoking point
than olive oil*

♥ *Baking* ♥
*it's a great vegan alternative
to butter*

♥ *Skin* ♥
*instead of silly expensive
chemical moisturisers*

♥ *Hair* ♥
*3 or 4 tablespoons into dry hair, wrap hair in cling film, lash on a hat
(heats up your head), leave in while you watch a trashy film and binge
on ice-cream, wash out and hello lovely soft hair!*

GROUND OR FLAKED ALMONDS

Cheap as chips when you get them in discount supermarkets. I use them instead of flour for baking and as a crumb topping on casseroles, and I blend flaked almonds to make almond milk (page 309).

FROZEN BERRIES

Because you know what? The fresh fellas are just crazy expensive in Ireland and half the pack is usually mouldy anyway! Frozen fellas are picked when they are actually ripe. I use them to make healthy jam (see my blog) and Raspberry Upside-Down Cake (page 222), I pop them in porridge (page 31), and sure, if you're feeling fancy, you can pop them in the bottom of a glass of Cava. Now check for yourself – occasionally they have health warnings saying you must cook them, but I've never been great at obeying that.

TINNED MIXED BEANS OR BUTTER BEANS

Sounds boring, right? Wrong! I usually have nearly a slab of these guys in my house. Use for Faked Baked Beans (page 125), Meatless Balls (page 151), White Bean and Mint Spread (page 281), Hummus (page 286) and whipping up a super-fast vegan chilli.

GLUTEN-FREE OATS

If you are what you eat, I may have spent some time in college as an oat ... That doesn't really make sense ... Anyhow, I usually have a few bags of GF oats knocking about the place. They're great for making bread (page 34), proats (pages 53-57) and Protein Pancakes (page 58) – also, if I'm really stuck for flour I blend up a cup of oats and sieve it. I keep the fine bit for flour, e.g. to make béchamel sauce, and keep the coarser bit to add to bread or use as a crumbly topping on something else.

Tips for Thrifty Healthy Eating

♥ DISCOUNT SUPERMARKETS ♥

Goods to get: all sorts of veg, frozen fruit, tinned beans, tinned fish, organic or free-range chickens, nuts and seeds, free-range eggs, honey, tea, coffee, buttermilk, organic milk
Star buys: maple syrup, chia seeds, pecan nuts

♥ ETHNIC MARKETS ♥

Goods to get: goji berries (sometimes known as boxthorn fruit), dates, spices, rice, cornmeal, herbs, tofu
Star buys: unusual fresh fruits (e.g. proper fresh coconuts with juice, papaya), unusual fresh veg (e.g. Jerusalem artichokes, taro root, plantains), also bamboo steamers for cooking, nice bowls, unusual sweets and treats

♥ FARMERS' MARKETS ♥

It's sad that in the modern era one's brain always assumes that the nice thing will cost more. For years when living in Galway I would peruse the St Nicholas market and look at all the gorgeous veggies and fruit, but then go off and buy their cheaper, blander counterparts in the supermarket. It was only after a lucky weekend and a fat pay cheque that I decided to treat myself and get all my fresh produce (fruit, veg, eggs) in the market. What the hell? It was half the price of what I got in the name-brand supermarkets.
Star buys: locally sourced fruits picked when they're properly ripened, max nutrition and super taste, seasonal veg, good chat

♥ REAL BUTCHERS ♥

Here you'll get better quality, good advice and more types of cuts of meat.
Star buy: tougher cuts of meat from the fore-quarter (e.g. beef) that can be cooked slowly at lower temperatures (delicious in stews, a good source of protein and much cheaper than more 'in demand' cuts)

♥ WHOLESALERS ♥

While I used to think you needed a wholesaler card to use them, often you just need cash in hand and a shopping list.
Star buys: grains, stock, pulses and frozen meat

♥ KEEP YOUR GLASS JARS ♥

My mother calls this my Protestant hoarding habit. It might sound a bit war era, but why do we spend loads of money for Tupperware that we damage, stain with tomato and lose the lid of when we are buying perfect, sterile containers as a bonus when we get stuff in jars? If you're good at not dropping things, big jars are great to bring your lunch to school or work, and tall, skinny ones are great for making your own salad dressing or infusing oils or extracts.

These ideas may sound silly, simple or obvious, but buying all my veggies and staples in a cheaper supermarket actually means I buy more organic stuff and more free-range items because I'm not spending a silly amount on basics like milk, grains, etc. Shopping in ethnic supermarkets exposes you to a more exciting array of spices, sauces and fresh produce. The market and butcher's can mean more seasonal, locally produced items and the wholesaler can make shopping for big families more manageable. It's so much easier to eat healthy when you're actually excited about your food!

Preserves, Sauces & Things that

Like to Live in Your Fridge

These are all the tasty bits and pieces to accompany the other recipes and new tricks you might be interested in mastering, such as pickling or making your own hummus. Think of them as the things that like to get sprinkled or poured on other stuff and that like to live in jars in your cupboard and fridge, just waiting to make your everyday meals tastier or perhaps even a little healthier.

Often it's that one unusual ingredient that makes a dish – like the preserved lemons on page 277 in Moroccan cuisine – or that topper or side that just makes a meal extra special.

This section is full of my odds, sods and bods: the best sauces for your dinners and desserts, the perfect sauerkraut (page 270) for an amazing hamburger or the classiest vanilla extract for top-notch baking (page 296).

Before jumping in to making something, have a peruse through this section. Are there any dips you'd like to add to your barbecue, any sweet sauces to make your breakfast or dessert more exciting?

Rosemary Stuffing

Perfect for the Christmas turkey or a roast chicken, this Christmas-scented
stuffing is also dairy free and can be made vegan with the substitutions
suggested in the recipe. Lots of folks actually use their stuffing as stuffing.
Imagine. That freaks me out so I cook mine in a dish alongside the turkey/
chicken or just make it for other things like the sandwich on page 109.

MAKES 3 CUPS (ABOUT 350G)

**2 cups (2 large handfuls) torn
up, slightly stale GF bread**

olive oil, for frying

½ red onion

¾ cup (120g) bacon lardons
leave out for vegan version

3 tbsp fresh rosemary, chopped

1 tbsp fresh thyme, chopped

pinch salt

few twists of pepper

1 egg *use 1 tbsp chia seeds and 3
tbsp water instead to make it vegan*

**½ cup (70g) black olives,
chopped**

1 Preheat the oven to 180°C.

2 Blitz your bread chunks in a food processor to make crumbs,
or tear them up as small as you can if you don't have a food
processor.

3 Finely chop the red onion.

4 Put a pan on a medium-high heat. When it's hot, lash in a glug
of olive oil. Sauté the onions and lardons until the onions are
soft.

5 In a bowl, mix the breadcrumbs, herbs, salt, pepper, lardons,
onion and egg.

6 If the mix feels a little dry, I add a tablespoon of olive oil or a
little water. But, generally speaking, I like my stuffing crumbly,
not moist, since I'm going to drown it in gravy later!

7 Pop the stuffing mix in a small oven dish, cover with tin foil
and place in the oven. Some folks would cover it with tin foil
but I like it a little crispy on top. Bake for 20–25 minutes,
depending on how brown you like your stuffing.

Croutons

This may not seem all that important, but I've been passing on croutons for a long time now – no crunch in soup, no crunch in Caesar salad. Sad little Finn. Anyway, since store-bought gluten-free bread ain't always the best, I never wanted to get my hopes up trying to make croutons and then being disappointed with the result. But one fateful day, after cutting all the crusts off a loaf of gluten-free bread to make Bold Bread and Butter Pudding (er mi gerd, try it – page 225), I decided to give them a go. Guess what? The gluten-free bread that even the dog won't eat (and generally speaking he eats everything) made the most delicious, crunchy, garlicky croutons!

1   Preheat the oven to 180°C, though these guys can be done at pretty much any temperature. (If I'm roasting any veg, I just put the croutons in at the same temp. If I don't want to use the oven, I just do them under the grill – careful when you do it this way: they need to be watched so they don't burn!)

2   Lay your little bread squares out on a baking tray, drizzle with olive oil, sprinkle with salt, rosemary and garlic powder. Swoosh them all around with your hands so they get evenly coated and pop them in the oven.

3   I leave them in for up to 20 minutes, giving them a mix at about 10 minutes so that they brown evenly. Basically, the longer you leave them the crunchier they will get. I like mine golden and not that crunchy!

MAKES 2 CUPS (ABOUT 200G)

2 cups (2 large handfuls) GF bread cut up into little squares *you can use just crusts if you need to use them up*

4 tbsp olive oil

1 tsp salt

1 tbsp fresh rosemary leaves

¼ tsp garlic powder

Preserves

There is something bizarrely satisfying about pickling and preserving. Not only does it feel like getting in touch with domestic practices of older, simpler times, it is also, for me, where my love of science and passion for food most get to mingle. I love thinking about the salt percentages for the perfect brine, the bacterial balance for a healthy gut and the alchemy-like transformation of a humble vegetable or fruit to something insanely tasty and healthy with a newly extended lifespan. To expand your knowledge of this wonderful skill, I highly recommend *The Cultured Club* by Dearbhla Reynolds.

Pickled Red Cabbage

I fell in love with the simplicity that is pickled cabbage in a wonderful alternative cafe in Dublin. They serve it on eggs and toast and I learned to make it on one of my favourite yoga retreats (called Fraoch) in the Gyreum Ecolodge. This is my own take on things, with a little less sugar and a little more sharpness. You can lash spices and things like mustard seed into this too, if you like, but I think the cabbage is pretty good at doing its own thing.

1   Slice your cabbage in half lengthways and, holding the chunky stalk bit, run it over a mandoline to get super-thin slices. If you don't have one, just try to shred it really fine. You get a nice texture that way and the pickle gets to work faster.

2   Have a tall sterilised glass jar with a tight-fitting lid ready to go – I like the ones with the rubber seal at the top. In a pot, bung your salt, sugar and vinegars and place on a low-medium heat until the salt and sugar dissolve. Then let it cool a bit. You don't want to lash it into the cabbage too hot or it'll lose its crunch!

3   Stuff all of your cabbage into the tall jar – it's OK if it's densely packed. When the vinegar mix is cool, pour it into the jar and put on the lid. Don't worry if all the cabbage isn't covered – you can just turn the jar over like an hourglass whenever you're in the kitchen and you remember.

4   I would generally make this mix, say, on a Friday evening and then have it ready for an insanely tasty Sunday brunch, but it's up to yourself and your levels of self-control.

TO SERVE

What kind of stuff would you put this recipe with? I freakin' love it on scrambled eggs and toast with a big pile of toasted seeds on top – a brunch of the highest order!

MAKES ROUGHLY A
2 LITRE JAR

1 large head red cabbage

½ cup (130g) salt

⅓ cup (75g) sugar

3 cups (720ml) pale vinegar
I use apple cider vinegar, a live one with the 'mother' still in it, extra awesome for your stomach!

½ tbsp different vinegar *I like a darker/sweeter variety to go with the dark red of the cabbage so a balsamic or red-wine vinegar would be nice*

Stupidly Simple Sauerkraut

I hope no German ever reads this bit, as I'm sure they would be completely horrified by something I'm doing here. But I love this recipe, it's super simple, it keeps for ages and I spoon a big scoop of it onto nearly everything. Obvious contenders would be hotdogs and hamburgers.

MAKES ROUGHLY A 1 LITRE JAR, DEPENDING ON THE SIZE OF YOUR CABBAGE

1 head white cabbage

salt *enough to sprinkle between each big handful of cabbage*

1   Crazy short ingredient list, right? It's insane something so simple can be so good!

2   Get your big head of cabbage and take off the outer leaves. These fellas are usually a bit muddy. Now take one or two of the clean outer leaves and set them aside for later.

3   Shred the cabbage the best way you know how. I cut it in half or thirds and use a mandoline to get lovely thin slivers – the thinner the better, as it creates more surface area for the good bacteria to work its magic. Sometimes fermenting feels like I'm back in a science lab! No worries if you don't have a fancy cutting device: just carefully cut super-thin slices with a knife.

4   Get a big colander, place it over a big bowl (you want to catch any 'juice', as you will need it later) and start layering your shredded cabbage into the colander with sprinkles of salt. Keep going till all the cabbage and salt are used up.

5   Leave for an hour or so to let it wilt a bit.

6   Next, cram all the cabbage into a big super-clean airtight jar. (I usually swirl the jar out with a good big splash of boiling water, being careful not to burn my hand on hot glass when pouring it out! I don't do full-on sterilising techniques, as this stuff usually gets eaten up in a few weeks.) Pour in any juice that was caught in the cabbage bowl. Next, tuck the cabbage leaves you set aside earlier around the shredded cabbage at the top of the jar. There should be a good bit of space left at the top.

7   It's important to put pressure on the cabbage so it releases its water and
    to keep it all submerged. I usually put a small, clean jam jar with heavy
    stuff in it – e.g. rocks – on top of the cabbage for the first few days to
    hold it down.

8   Nearly there! Next cover your jar with a clean piece of J-cloth or tea
    towel and secure with some string on a rubber band. You should still
    be able to do this with the little weighted jar inside. Pop the jar in the
    cupboard and let it work its magic for a few days. The temperature
    of the room will affect fermentation time. For me, in a fairly cold
    house on the west coast of Ireland, it takes three days. So it could be
    less in warmer places. When your sauerkraut is to your taste and it's
    completely submerged in liquid, take out the weight, put on the lid and
    pop the jar in the fridge. You're ready to go.

TO SERVE

I put this on everything: in salads, on the bean balls on page 151 with the
beef burgers on page 163 or on hotdogs, too, for classic Canadian summer-
holiday memories!

Stupidly Simple Saeurkraut, page 270

Pickled Red Cabbage, page 269

Cucumber Pickles

Every Canada Day my family have a massive barbecue. All the in-laws and out-laws are there. There's a huge table of amazing food that everyone has prepared and a big barbecue being manned out in the garden with plenty of burgers cooking away. As far as I'm concerned, a burger ain't a burger unless it's drowned in mustard and topped with pickles. These little fellas can be prepped a few days before you need them and keep for a week or so. Though I've been known to munch on them the very next day.

MAKES ROUGHLY A 500ML JAR

1 large fresh cucumber

1 tbsp sea salt or pink Himalayan

1½ cups (350ml) cooled boiled water

2 cloves garlic

½ tsp black peppercorns

1 tsp mustard seeds

2 bay leaves *1 is fine: I just love the taste*

1   Cut the ends off your cucumbers. It's important not to put them in the jar, as they can make the pickles lose their crispiness. Slice the cucumbers lengthways, as thin as you like – I do them super fine with a mandoline, and you could also use a vegetable peeler.

2   In a cup, make your brine by dissolving the salt in the water.

3   In a cleaned jar – rinse with boiling water – layer up your ingredients. I tend to put the garlic cloves at the bottom and then layer up the cucumber slices with the peppercorns and mustard seeds. Finally, push the bay leaves down the sides of the jar, pour over the brine and put on the lid. Keep in the fridge.

TO SERVE

If you're making the sauerkraut (page 270) at the same time, steal one of the white cabbage leaves and use this to cover the pickles and brine. The happy bacteria on the surface of the cabbage leaf will complement your pickles.

After a day's fermenting, you're good to go. Keep it in the fridge and enjoy on top of burgers (like on page 163) or on salads (page 100)

Preserved Lemons

I fell in love with preserved lemons a few years ago at a yoga weekend. To be honest, I can't even remember what they were served with – I was just eating them out of the jar and making that face you make when you eat sour sweets. I implore you to make them! Preserved lemons taste like nothing else on earth and they add a wonderful umami kick to food – great for vegans, as this flavour often comes from meat.

1 Top and tail the 4 unwaxed lemons and cut them into super-thin slices.

2 In a clean jar – I wash a pasta-sauce jar thoroughly and then rinse with boiling water (using a dish cloth to protect my hands) – layer up the lemon slices, salt, peppercorns, coriander seeds and bay leaves until all your ingredients are gone.

3 Pour the extra lemon juice into the jar. Using a spoon – sometimes I use the bottom of a rolling pin – press the lemon slices down so they are covered by the juice.

TO SERVE

Most preserved lemons take yonks to be ready, but by using slices instead of wedges we speed the whole process up! The surface area available for the reaction is massively increased and so in a warm kitchen you could start getting some use out of these bad boys after a week! I label the jar with some masking tape to note the date I made them. When they're ready, they'll have a much darker appearance and a very savoury, umami taste.

Before you use a slice for a recipe, just give it a quick rinse to get rid of the excess salt.

Preserved lemons give the mystery kick to tagine, but also try them in the hummus on page 286, or add about $^1/_2$ tsp (or more for the brave) of them mashed to a blended salad dressing or a little into any meaty stew.

MAKES ROUGHLY A 400ML JAR

4 unwaxed lemons plus juice of 2 more

sea salt or pink Himalayan salt *enough to sprinkle a good bit between each layer of lemon chunks and to top the jar*

½ tsp black peppercorns

1 tsp coriander seeds

2 bay leaves

Sauces

Since one of the most poxy parts of gluten-free sabotage in meals is the sauces (the meat could be fine, the veg could be fine), I thought it was important to have a saucy little section all on its own. So when you make your dish and you think, *what will I put on this?* you can just turn to this page! I've included both savoury and sweet sauces so you're covered for dinner *and* dessert.

Béchamel Sauce

So simple but so good! Conquering the humble béchamel was a rite of passage on my culinary course, and now that I know how to make it properly from scratch, I could never again buy it in a jar from the supermarket.

1 Since this classic French sauce cooks fast, I like to have all my ingredients measured out and sitting there ready to go.

2 Put a small pot on a medium-high heat and let it get nice and hot. When you feel the heat when waving your hand over the top, chuck in the butter. I like to lift the pot off the heat and shimmy the butter around in a super-fast circular motion. This way it doesn't burn on one bit of the pot, but it does get a little brown and that adds awesome flavour.

3 When the butter is melted, chuck in your flour and stir like mad with a small wooden spoon. Here you are cooking the flour out a little bit in the butter – you should be getting a nice smell – and then as soon as it starts to bubble lash in the milk!

4 Shimmy it all around, stirring like mad and, after 3 minutes of simmering and stirring, you should end up with a sauce that is on the runny side of thick, which is exactly where I like it – add more milk if you want something thinner.

5 Next, mix in your mustard, twist in your pepper and grate in your nutmeg. I'm a little heavy handed on the nutmeg so it could be as much as $^1/_2$ a tsp but it's hard to tell when you're grating. Trust your own tastes.

MAKES 2 CUPS OF RUNNY-THICK SAUCE

1 tbsp butter

1 heaped tbsp GF plain flour

1 $\frac{1}{2}$ cups (360ml) milk

pinch salt

1 tsp Dijon mustard *for a cool polka-dot-looking sauce I sub in 2 tsp of wholegrain mustard*

twist of pepper *use white pepper if you don't want the flecks of black and brown*

pinch nutmeg

TO SERVE

Cauliflower just loves this sauce. Lightly steam some cauliflower chunks, pop them in a casserole dish, smother with this sauce and grate over some mature cheese. Bake at 200°C for 20–30 minutes for the ultimate comfort food. I also use this sauce for tuna pasta bakes. Cook 2 cups (125g) of penne pasta, mix in 1 tin of pole-and-line-caught tuna, all of this sauce recipe and grate cheese over the top. Bake for 15–20 minutes at 200°C.

Herby Tomato Sauce

This is good for pasta or the lasagne on page 160.

MAKES 4–5 SERVINGS

½ **white onion**

1 **tbsp olive oil**

½ **tsp oregano**

½ **tsp herbes de Provence or dried basil and oregano**

splash red wine

400g tinned plum tomatoes

½ **tsp tamari soy sauce**

salt and pepper, to taste

1   Finely chop the onion. Put a small pot on a medium to high heat. When it's hot, lash in the olive oil and a little piece of onion. When it sizzles, add in the rest of the onion. Sauté until soft.

2   Add the herbs and the red wine. When the wine has cooked off a little add the tinned tomato and tamari.

3   Allow the sauce to simmer away on a low heat for up to an hour. Depending on the type of tinned tomatoes, I sometimes add a splash of balsamic vinegar to give some sweetness.

TO SERVE

It's lovely as it is, but sometimes I blend it with a hand blender to make a smooth sauce for things like pizzas and pasta bakes.

White Bean and Mint Spread

This one came about when I wanted hummus but didn't have chickpeas. I've said before that I think it's nuts how much we spend on groceries when there is so much high-quality, better-value food out there that just needs a bit more love to prep. When I'm in a big supermarket, I always pick up a few bags of ground almonds, tinned tomatoes and different kinds of tinned cooked beans. That way there's always something in reserve if I suddenly need a load of them for a recipe, and I don't have to feel like I spent a fortune just to make one cake/dip/loaf of bread! Chances are nearly everything will already be in my kitchen.

Phew, major sidetrack there – you were just here for the dip!
So this is amazeballs with the likes of falafel, on a burger, spread in a wrap with salad and chicken or used as a dip with crudités (yeah, that's a fancy word for sticks of raw veg).

1   In a bowl – or the mini-chopper for the hand blender, if yours comes with one – add all the ingredients and blend until smooth.
2   Lash into an airtight container and into the fridge.
3   This keeps well for quite a few days.

MAKES ROUGHLY 400G

400g tinned white butter beans

5 tbsp (75ml) olive oil

½ lemon, juice only

2 tbsp fresh mint leaves, chopped

½ tsp garlic powder

salt, to taste

French Dressing

**The absolute classic dressing, French in name but multinational in use. I
actually love this dressing on the typical Greek salad of feta, olives, cucumber,
tomato and red onion.**

MAKES ABOUT ⅓ CUP (80ML)

3 cloves roasted garlic or 1 raw

**⅓ cup (70ml) good quality
olive oil**

3 tbsp apple cider vinegar

salt and pepper, to taste

3 tsp Dijon mustard *use less if
you don't like it too hot*

squeeze of lemon juice

Peel and crush the garlic. Add all the ingredients to a clean glass
jar, close the lid tightly and shake. Voilà – all done! The longer you
leave it, the more deliciously garlicky it will become. Only put it
in the fridge if you absolutely have to, as the coldness of the fridge
can make it go semi-solid!

Chilli and Lime Sauce

This one's great for the Irish Malaysian Noodle Soup (page 144) but also works well with any stir-fry dish.

1 Deseed and finely chop all the chillies. Be super-careful not to touch your eyes when you're handling the chillies – they burn! Juice the limes.

2 Crush the chilli, lime juice and sugar using a pestle and mortar (or, if you don't have one, using a tablespoon in a bowl). Transfer the sauce to a small jar. The sauce is best if left to stew for a few hours, but it's still good if you can't wait.

MAKES 1 SMALL JAR (ABOUT 100ML)

3 red chillies

1 green chilli

1 large or 2 small limes

1 tbsp fine brown sugar or honey

Roast Garlic and Preserved Lemon Hummus

I love this dip for crackers but it also works great in a wrap or with falafel.

MAKES ROUGHLY A 300ML JAR

400g tinned chickpeas

1 tbsp preserved lemon (page 277)

3 cloves roasted garlic *go to whatever your garlic delight levels are: I just use 3*

4 tbsp olive oil *I add more if the mix is feeling a little dry: up your lemon quantity too*

2 tbsp lemon juice

3 tbsp tahini

salt, to taste

1 Drain the chickpeas and give them a quick rinse under the tap.

2 Take some preserved lemon and mush it up with a fork. This recipe also works wonderfully without the preserved lemons – I just happen to be a bit obsessed with them!

3 Peel the skin off the roasted garlic. It's super simple to make this – whenever you do any kind of roast veg just chuck a few cloves of garlic, with their skin on, into the mix and they'll get soft, squishy and a little smoky! Once roasted, they keep in the fridge for about a week. Also some folks find it a bit difficult to digest raw garlic so this is a great way to get the classic garlic hit without the rumbly tummy afterwards.

4 If you have a snazzy food processor you can lash everything in at this point. I'm happy using a hand blender – at this point you might've noticed it's an extension of my arm – set to high speed to do the mixing. If the mix feels a little dry, just add another tablespoon or two of olive oil and another squeeze of lemon.

5 Store in an airtight container in the fridge for about three days – don't forget to label it with the date!

Almond Vegan Paleo Pesto

I developed this pesto so I could enjoy my own fresh version without the hassle or expense of a food processor.

MAKES 1 JAR (ROUGHLY 200G)

1 cup (120g) flaked almonds
1 cup (30g) baby leaf spinach
½ cup (20g) fresh basil leaves
½ cup (120ml) lemon juice
⅓ cup (80ml) olive oil
1 tsp garlic powder

1 Soak the flaked almonds for a few hours in some cold water. This softens them up, making them easier to blend and giving the pesto a smoother consistency.

2 Drain them and pat them dry in a clean tea towel – this stops the pesto being too watery.

3 In a hand-blender-friendly jug, add the spinach, basil, almond flakes, lemon juice, olive oil and garlic powder.

4 Simple as! Just blend it all up and have a little taste – you might want a little more lemon (if it feels a bit oily) or a little more olive oil (if it's a bit too sharp).

5 You can add some salt to taste as well – I don't if I'm using it in a recipe that already has salt. This keeps well for up to a week (if not longer) in a clean glass jar in the fridge.

TO SERVE

It's an integral part of the Siren Sea Spaghetti on page 148, but it also works wonders with other pasta dishes, in wraps and sambos or as a salad dressing if you add it to $^1/_2$ cup (120ml) olive oil and $^1/_3$ cup (80ml) lemon juice.

Tequila-less Salsa

This salsa is so much fresher and more colourful then those store-bought nasties. It's called Tequila-less because everyone in my family seems to lash booze into salsa for some reason. This is the more saintly version of a barbecue staple.

1   Finely chop your onion, pepper and tomatoes and pop them all in a bowl.
2   Squeeze over the lime juice, season with salt and pepper and lash in a bit of Tabasco.
3   Finely chop your fresh coriander and sprinkle it over the bowl.

SERVES 4 AS A SIDE

½ **red onion**

1 yellow bell pepper *you can use other colours if you like; I just don't like them raw*

6 big tomatoes or, like, 20 little fellas

1 big lime or ½ lemon and ½ lime

salt and pepper, to taste

few lashes Tabasco

big handful fresh coriander *that's cilantro to our friends across the pond*

Dracula-Friendly Guac

Have you ever longed for guacamole in a restaurant, paid the 'guac is extra' charge and then been served up something that's more onion and garlic than avocado? Turn yourself into a vamp magnet with this low-to-no garlic guacamole!

SERVES 4 AS A SIDE

3 ripe avocados

¼ red onion – super-finely chopped

8 red cherry tomatoes *if you find green or yellow ones, that would look so much cooler!*

1 lime

sprinkling of garlic powder, if you are so inclined

salt and pepper, to taste

dash of Tabasco sauce (optional)

1. Cut the avocados in half. Take out the stones. Scoop the insides into a big bowl and mash.

2. Finely chop your onion and tomatoes and lash them in the bowl.

3. Squeeze in your lime juice, sprinkle over the garlic and add the salt and pepper to taste. If you like a bit of heat, add the Tabasco.

Berry Couli-ish

Since I shudder in horror at the amount of sugar that goes into coulis before they grace the dessert plate or mysteriously end up at the breakfast table, I devised my own simple version that can be whipped up in minutes and won't leave your teeth feeling fuzzy.

MAKES 400ML

3 cups (400g) frozen berries of your choice *e.g. blueberries, raspberries or mixed forest fruits*

3 tbsp honey or maple syrup

1 If you're naughty like me and bung way too many things in the microwave, you can pop your berries in a big bowl and lash them on high until they are all steamy and hot through.

2 If you don't want to do that, you can heat them up in a pot – just be sure that you don't let the ones on the bottom burn.

3 Let them cool a bit, lash them in a tall jug or something you can get a hand blender into and blitz until smooth. Add your chosen form of sweetness and do another quick blitz.

TO SERVE

This is insanely tasty over crumble and as a colourful companion to custard or, in the morning, over your porridge, granola, yogurt, etc. It keeps well in a sealed container in the fridge for up to a week.

Cardamom and Vanilla Apple Sauce

I adore this sauce – it's wonderful in the morning with yogurt or on top of porridge. I also like to make a plain version of it, which is very handy for sweetening other sauces like the tomato sauce on page 280 or the cranberry sauce on page 295.

1 Peel and chop the apples. Put a big pot on a medium–high heat and lash in the apples. If they look a little dry, add a splash of water. Put a lid on the pot and reduce to a medium temperature.

2 Crush and open the cardamom pods. Crush the seeds you find inside using a mortar and pestle (or in a plastic bag with a rolling pin if you're stuck).

3 Split open the vanilla pod and scrape out the seeds. Don't throw away the pod. You could add it to a container of sugar to infuse and make vanilla sugar or you can add it to the pot here – just make sure to take it out before you blend the apple sauce.

4 Add the crushed cardamom, vanilla seeds and maple syrup to the apple pot. Stew for up to 40 minutes on a low heat.

5 When the apples are very soft, take them off the heat and allow them to cool. Blend with a hand blender until smooth.

TO SERVE

I keep this in a big glass jar in the fridge and it usually stays good for up to 2 weeks.

MAKES A 1 LITRE JAR TO LIVE OFF FOR A WEEK

10 large cooking apples

2 cardamom pods

1 vanilla pod

3 tbsp maple syrup *you can leave this out if you use eating apples instead of cooking ones*

Banana Sauce

Disclaimer out there right away: this one isn't for everyone. One of my dad's mates used to make this in London back in the early nineties. I have fond memories of sitting on the fire escape of the apartment in the summer time, stuffing our faces with croissants, and I'd be allowed a tiny bowl of coffee that was really mostly milk. This sauce is delish on croissants and any other random sweet thing that might be a little dry – e.g. a breakfast muffin or a slice of carrot cake.

SERVES 4

3 large ripe bananas

1 tbsp maple syrup *optional if you feel the bananas are sweet enough*

½ tsp cinnamon

¼ or less tsp nutmeg

Peel the bananas, break into bits and pop in a bowl. Add the maple syrup and spices to taste and mash well with a fork. Spoon onto whatever baked good you want to jazz up.

Cranberry Sauce

For me the jury is out on whether this is savoury or sweet. It's the best friend of turkey and cheese, but I also like to put it with porridge and on yogurt. You can decide for yourself and also tinker with the sweetness according to your own tastes!

1   Wash your cranberries and bung them in a pot. Slowly cook them on a medium-low heat for half an hour. Add the apples if they aren't in sauce form – otherwise, don't add the apple sauce till the cranberries have cooked more.

2   When the mix has all gone nice and soft, start to add your sweetness. Taste a few times as you add to see how much tang vs sweet you like.

3   Allow the sauce to cool and store in sealed containers in the fridge (it keeps for a few days). This makes an awesome little present at Christmas time – if you're visiting someone else's house for the big dinner, you could bring this along, with a ribbon around the jar, as a gift.

MAKES 600ML

1 big bag (400g) fresh cranberries

1 cup (250g) apple sauce *just add 2 peeled and chopped eating apples if you don't have any sauce*

4 tbsp brown sugar or honey

Gin Bourbon Vanilla Extract

So let's talk about a sexy little thing that gets a bad rep these days: vanilla. Long hailed as another word for boring (and strangely pale, considering the pods are dark brown), it's one of my favourite flavours when done right. But I'm not happy paying a bajillion euro for teeny bottles of shop-bought extract, and I feel guilty giving healthy people the cheap shite made of chemical flavouring in corn syrup. So have a think about it: the good stuff is booze plus vanilla pods. I have booze; vanilla pods aren't that pricey: bingo!

MAKES 240ML

1 cup (240ml) booze that's not too overpowering *I've chosen gin since I can make G&Ts with the leftovers*

as many vanilla pods as you're willing to pay for *I use 4 but 8 would be amazing*

a pretty 300ml glass bottle

also a funnel to get it in the bottle

1 So here's what you do …

2 Pick your booze. For super thriftiness, you could try to use whatever spirits you've got in your house – a decent vodka or brandy would work well too.

3 Get your vanilla pods, cut a slit down the middle of them, then cut them in half (this is for when the bottle gets a little empty – you want them to stay covered). The more the merrier for a more intense flavour!

4 Then, simple as pie, put the vanilla pods in the glass bottle and use your funnel to pour in the booze!

5 Screw the lid on tight and label to your heart's content – putting the date that you made it on it makes it easier to know when it's ready. The flavour will take up to 8 weeks to develop (though you could use it after a minimum of 3 – judge for yourself by the flavour) and will be unique depending on the type of alcohol and vanilla you use. I like Irish gin and bourbon vanilla – just because the name is confusing. It keeps indefinitely, and the colour and flavour intensity will change over time. If you're giving it as a gift, note that it should get a shake every week or so.

TOP TIP
While you always hear that alcohol 'cooks off' because the boiling point of ethanol is just under 80°C, this may not be completely true, due to alcohol's ability to form compounds with other ingredients in your baking. Plainly speaking, don't serve it to people who are off the sauce or put it in a raw dessert if you don't want a boozy flavour! Vanilla seeds scraped out of the pod work lovely in baking and are the little dark speckles you see in high-quality vanilla ice-cream.

Why I Exercise

I could harp on about this for days so I will keep it short.
The fastest way to hate exercising (I think) is to do it for
a 'bikini body' or looks. I run to clear my mind, I surf for
fun and adrenaline, I do yoga to unwind and I lift weights
to feel strong and relieve tension and anger. Exercising
is never a struggle because I'm only choosing it for good
reasons. If you don't like a type of exercise, don't do it.
I hate cardio machines in the gym, so I get most of my
cardio from surfing or running for buses. Pilates is too
expensive for me at the moment so I do yoga at home (or
on the beach, for that matter).

Considering it's such a physical thing, I think it's
funny that I exercise for mental reasons – stress relief,
uplifted mood and a break from everything that's
bothering me. I feel, when you look at it this way,
the physical manifestations are just an added bonus
– weight management, better skin and an improved
immune system!

Using YouTube as a Personal Trainer

If you're not into reading heavy tomes of nutritional advice, or you haven't quite got the cash for that fitness class or personal training session, it's literally all waiting for you online! Below I've listed some of my favourite YouTubers and why they're so darn helpful. I will save you the gushy moment about how listening to TEDx Talks via YouTube actually helped me figure out what I wanted to do with my life.

Don't just sit and watch the videos mindlessly — listen to them with earphones while you're out shopping, use the cooking demos like an in-house personal chef or the fitness videos as a trainer in your living room.

I haven't listed the full complement of folks I follow because it's easy to get overloaded with info, but try these guys on for size and find your own new gurus as well.

✻ TONE IT UP ✻

This was a major fave of mine when I started college. I had already done a few years in the gym but with trainers who really weren't passionate about their jobs or interested enough to look at the whole picture of exercise, recovery and diet. More one for the girls, these ladies offer fitness videos covering kettlebells, basic weight training, high-intensity interval training and loads of other stuff. If you need it, they even have a monthly schedule and challenges to keep you motivated. They were the big 'ah ha' moment for me of putting nutrition, cardio, weights and relaxation all together to be a happy, healthy human!

✻ LEAN SECRETS ✻

Another one that I found early on. I just love Brenda's videos and amazing recipes! She also has a couple of ebooks. Often healthy dishes can be seriously sad-looking versions of their usual selves, so it's refreshing that every single one of her dishes I've tried has been amazing. I'm usually quite uppity and change recipes around a bit but hers are perfect as they are! Her nutrition chat and recipes are great for guys too – some other fitness ladies can be geared much more towards women when they talk about food.

✻ NIKKI BLACKKETTER ✻

Such a little sweetie – I watch her videos with the rapt attention college students in Ireland reserve for *Home and Away*. While generally documenting her life and career, she has great content for those interested in competing in bikini competitions.

✻ LAIRD HAMILTON ✻

Considered a god among men by a lot of the surfing community, Laird is a big wave surfer from Hawaii and has amazing content on training, surfing and diet. His wife, Gabrielle Reece, also has a fantastic book that I'd recommend for women.

✻ STEVE COOK ✻

I swear I don't watch him just because he's pretty ... One for the bodybuilders, or those getting into weight training – he's great for motivation chat, diet and exercise from a man's perspective. He is also good fun and not so scarily intense as other bodybuilding gurus can be.

Drin

ks

As a hyperactive mad woman, spending my days running around all over the place and usually doing some kind of sport, it is so important to stay hydrated. With that said, water for me is the main man. Anything else is kind of a treat, so here I've included my favourite coffee recipes that I use for a little zip first thing in the morning and for that 11 a.m. slump, as well as the almond milk (page 309) that is so amazing by itself or in your coffee or baking!

And finally a few of my favourite treats, both hot and cold, when you need something a little sweet.

Getting the Water into Ya!

I spend lots of my 'research hours' reading books and magazines, watching TED Talks and YouTube videos and listening to podcasts – all on the subjects of fitness and nutrition. Everybody's got their jam, but that's what I like!

The one very universal theme is that we need to drink more water. Not sports drinks, not coffee, not tea or juices: water. Since I've found it hard to remember since my undergrad days (it's easier when there's a water machine in your study room and in the gym), here are a few things I've discovered along the way to help me stay hydrated!

Disclaimer: I'm not saying you have to force water down your gullet or drink x amount of water per kg of bodyweight or anything like that. Generally I trust my body to let me know what it needs – the problem is that sometimes I'm so busy I don't notice until I'm terribly, terribly thirsty with no water on me!

COLD CLIMATE

I dunno about you, but I think it's easy to remember to drink water if you're in, say, the tropics. Ireland in the dead of winter – maybe not so much! When I was doing my MSc year, our building was a converted brewery in Cork and they had to keep a lot of the building cold for dissection rooms (delightful) and for the fish tanks (fair enough). Consequently, I never wanted to drink cold water, but I was so thirsty! Herbal teas, folks. I by no means find herbal teas an adequate replacement for my normal cup of tea (I am Irish, after all) but they were perfect to replace cold water. Getting up to make one was a chance to stretch my legs when stuck at a desk and having a Thermos of the stuff in lectures always reminded me to use it! Favourites include Pukka and Yogi teas.

MISSING YOUR FIZZY FELLAS

Inspired by my good friend Louise's night-out drink, the Skinny Bitch (vodka, sparkling water and fresh lime juice), I realised that lime and sparkling water are lovely on their own too. I'm not saying it's going to give you the sugar rush you're after, but it is a tasty, zingy pick-me-up!

BUT WATER IS BORING

Luckily I don't suffer from this one. My parents conditioned me from a young age, with juice only as a treat and water in my baba bottle. But if you really do find plain water boring, find ways to spice it up that don't involve chemical cordials and tonnes of sugar. Good combos are lemon and lime slices, lemon and cucumber (nearly a G&T!), crushed raspberries or the juice of 1 fresh squeezed orange to 1 litre of water. Play with your own favourite flavours! Herbal teas (yeah, they're back again) can work too. Once while studying I forgot about my tea and absentmindedly drank it, like, two hours later when it was cold. Turns out I like peppermint tea better that way. Try adding cold herbal teas, plus some ice and mint leaves, to your water bottle.

FOR CAFFEINE FIENDS

It's funny how certain countries just miss the memo sometimes. I was having a coffee with my cousin from Austria a few years back and he was horrified to find that we don't automatically serve a glass of water with coffee in Ireland. As the oh-so-reasonable Austrians know, coffee is a diuretic and therefore dehydrates the body. This, you know, gives you headaches and makes your skin look dry. Simple answer – when you make your cup of joe in the morning, train yourself to also pour yourself a glass of H_2O!

Pillowcase Almond Milk

After watching lots of wonderful YouTubers making delicious-looking almond milk with Vitamixes, food processors and muslin bags, I decided to have a crack at it myself. I'd been a bit bored with my coffee and thought almond protein coffee would be pretty slick. However, I had no plans to leave my house and go to Mothercare in search of muslin, be seen by friends' mothers and start rumours about being 'up the Damien' – preggo to non-Irish folk – and I also didn't feel like investing beyond my already well-loved hand blender.

So after some messing about and lots of giggling about bags that look like cow udders, I perfected my insanely simple recipe and was smugly offering guests homemade almond milk for their porridge and coffees. I implore, no, I demand that you try this recipe – it will make all those store-bought almond milks seem junky and wildly expensive and it's simple as anything and cheap as chips! The bits and bobs you will need are: weighing scales, normal cereal-type bowl, plate to cover, 2 big jugs, a hand blender, clean cotton pillowcase (or muslin if you're feeling fancy) and storage bottle with a swing top – think of the ones that lemonades come in.

1   1¼ cups (100g) flaked almonds is enough to make about 600ml of not-too-thick almond milk. I only make this much at a time, as it keeps for five days and that's all I need for porridge and coffees. If you drink more milk/have a big family just double the ingredients!

2   Pop the almonds in a bowl and pour in enough water to cover them. Stick a plate over the bowl as a lid (I don't like cling film very much – unnecessary plastic). If the weather's warm, I'll pop it in the fridge for 6 hours to overnight; in winter I'll leave it on the counter.

MAKES 500–600ML

1¼ cups (100g) flaked almonds *skins already off, folks, and these lads can be got in Aldi or Lidl for next to nothing*

3 cups (700ml) filtered water, plus more for soaking the almonds

2 tbsp maple syrup

pinch sea salt – I also use pink Himalayan

3   Once your lovely almonds are all soaked, lash them and their soaking water into a big jug and add the 3 cups (700ml) of water, the maple syrup and a pinch of salt. Blendy, blendy, blendy with the hand blender till it goes from bitty-looking water to smooth and milky – you even get a lovely bit of foam on the top. I noticed recently that the blender even makes a slightly different sound when it's done (less aggressive).

4   Now for the fun bit, where you won't want to make eye contact with anyone!

5   Get your pillow case and put one of its closed corners into the second clean jug. Pour the almond milk mix into the pillow case. Once it's all poured in, gently lift the pillowcase over the jug. You'll see milk pouring out udder-style, and once it slows down, squeeze the pillowcase from the top down to get the last of the milk out. You'll be left with a big handful of almond meal in the pillowcase (see the top tip below for what you can do with it).

6   Ta-dah – you now have almond milk! Decant it (oh, fancy word, Finn) into the swing-top bottle and into the fridge it goes. Almond milk will keep for about 5 days this way and is great in hot drinks, for breakfasts or to use in dairy-free, vegan and paleo baking. Have fun!

TOP TIP

From the videos I've seen, everyone seems to chuck the almond meal away, which seems terribly wasteful. The majority of the taste and healthy fats may be in the milk but the almond meal is perfect for gluten-free and paleo baking, as you can use it as a substitute for flour. Since it's a bit waterlogged at this point, I just pop it in the freezer in a plastic container until I need it. When I want to use it – e.g. for the cheesecake base on page 215 – I just take it out and toast it on a pan until it's dry and golden brown. Voilà – no waste!

Middle Eastern Cardamom Coffee

During my culinary course, I made the most of the wonderful foodie library that St Angela's had to offer. As well as the classics of Mary Berry, they also had weird and wonderful old books, from 1940s housewives' recipes to books on the history of coffee. An absolute caffeine fiend myself, I was fascinated by the ways that different countries go about their daily brew – the Turks serve it grounds still in; the Moroccans won't serve it without a sweet nibble to accompany it – but no matter the country, there was always the same reverence around the coffee ritual.

One of my favourite ideas was to add spices to the coffee. I never really liked the cinnamon-sprinkled-over-coffee idea (I was doing this a few years ago in a mad-cap attempt to control sugar cravings: sugar – 1 Finn – 0). It always just seemed to end up in bitty clumps. But the answer was nigh! Put the flavour in when you brew, not after, numpty!

1 I think the little moka pots (the ones where you put the water in the bottom, the ground beans in the middle and the coffee magically appears at the top) work best for this recipe, as the cardamom gets a chance to infuse the coffee while the water is steaming away.

2 Fill the wee bit at the bottom with water and pop in the ground-coffee-holding bit. On a wooden board, flatten your cardamom pods with the flat edge of a knife. This will pop the pod open and squash the seeds a bit to release flavour. Now take the seeds out and crush them in a mortar and pestle.

3 Put 1 tablespoon of the coffee in the grounds-holding piece and then pop in the squished cardamom seeds and then the rest of the coffee.

MAKES ONE CUP OF COFFEE TO TRANSPORT YOU TO THE LEVANT

1 cup (235ml) filtered water *or just generally non-freaky water*

2 cardamom pods, seeds removed and crushed, pods discarded *if you have a coffee grinder, just chuck these in when you're grinding the beans*

2 tbsp of your favourite ground coffee *extra points for grinding your own coffee from the beans!*

1 tsp sweetness *I've been using coconut palm sugar as a li'l treat to myself while I write, but that shizz is expensive: honey would do great too!*

4   Screw the lid on tight and put the coffee pot on the smallest ring of
    your stove. Using the ring that best fits the size of your pot (in general)
    is a better use of electricity and kinder to your wallet!

5   When the angry gurgling noise is over, your coffee is done. I've noticed
    the time on this varies wildly with the size of the pot, the hotness of
    the stove and the temp of the water you put in in the first place.
    So go by ear.

6   Put your sweetness in a cup and top with your tasty infused coffee.
    I drink mine black, but that's up to you. Go forth into the world a less
    sleepy, less grumpy human!

Chilli Hot Chocolate

I remember watching Juliette Binoche in *Chocolat* when I was little, and Mom and I dreaming that we were in that little chocolate shop in France drinking the Mayan delight. This is a simplified version, and ever since getting the hot chocolate flakes from Cocouture in Belfast, I just can't go back to the powder. This is one of those times where the ingredients are a little more expensive. So quality, not quantity, people – have beautiful real hot chocolate, just have it less often!

1 Let's do it the good old-fashioned way, folks – on the stove! Pour half of the milk into a small pot over a medium heat. As it begins to heat up, add your chilli – you want to give it time to infuse into the milk.

2 Next add the chocolate flakes and stir continuously to stop the chocolate sticking to the bottom and burning.

3 Add the rest of the milk and heat until steamy but not simmering – over-cooked milk is yacky!

TO SERVE

Nada! This hot chocolate relies on its own strength – it doesn't need cream or marshmallows to back it up. It's great with biscotti dipped in, though, or the churros from page 69.

SERVES 2 ON A COLD, DARK DAY IN NEED OF SPICY SUNSHINE

2 cups (470ml) organic full-fat cow's milk

pinch good quality chilli powder *you're not going to get the taste if it's old*

6 heaped tbsp hot chocolate flakes *more if you want, I like the Italian-style hot chocolate you can practically walk on. Try any good chocolate shop or even make your own by grating a Green & Black's chocolate bar*

a little brown sugar to taste (optional) *if you've got a serious sweet tooth*

Beefcake Coffee

I'd like to blame a fast metabolism, but whatever it is, no matter how massive my breakfast I just have to have something by 11 a.m. A little trick I found a while ago, when I didn't have any protein treats to hand (and didn't want to give into a sugary coffee), was to add a half or whole scoop of my favourite vanilla protein to my caffeine hit of the day.

This recipe is also great if you've already incorporated whey protein into your diet but are getting seriously bored of protein shakes. Here I've added quick and simple directions that will put a spring in your step and help you fight off the sweet-tooth demons while those around you are tucking into a muffin with coffee!

MAKES 1 HIGH-PROTEIN
CAFFEINE TURBO INJECTION

milk *I go full fat organic cow's milk*

favourite coffee *I like a medium roast Arabica*

vanilla whey protein *I'm currently a huge fan of Optimum Nutrition's 'Bourbon Vanilla', but also really like Kinetica's vanilla too – any good-quality whey protein will do*

1 Brew your chosen type of coffee – I make enough for one with a personal-sized, teeny moka pot: two hefty tablespoons will put a little hair on your chest. Make it with less water and nice and strong to get that double-espresso feel.

2 Fill a mug with milk and pour most of that into a little pot to heat up. Warm up over a medium heat.

3 Pour your protein in with the cold milk and mix to make a paste. Add the warmed milk and mix again.

4 Pour on your brewed coffee and you have the perfect caffeine-and-protein pick-me-up for the 11 a.m. slump!

5 If you're not a dairy fan, or just trying to cut back, this recipe works really well with my homemade almond milk (page 309) and you could also try using a vegan protein blend instead of whey.

Sangria

This is a simple version that I like to make in summer – perfect for large groups.

Just mix it all together and you're good to go!

DISCLAIMER:

The booze mysteriously gets soaked up by the fruit – don't let kids eat it!

1 bottle red wine

500ml–1l 7-Up Free

1 carton (1 litre) orange juice

3 shots brandy

4 shots Cointreau

loads of fruit to top it off

I usually go for orange slices, green grapes sliced in half and any other fruit I can get my hands on. Banana didn't work. Grapefruit would probably be too bitter!

Watermelon Slushie

While slushies in the college days were associated with neon-dyed, high-sugar tubes that may or may not have been spiked with vodka, this little fella is of the more saintly variety. With no added sugar or colouring whatsoever, it is the perfect pick-me-up on a hot summer's day. What you decide to do with it in the evening is entirely up to you (rum, the answer is always rum).

MAKES 4–6 LARGE GLASSES, DEPENDING ON THE SIZE OF YOUR WATERMELON

1 watermelon *yep, that simple! I find the smaller ones less inclined to have the big seeds, so getting a few of the wee ones means less cowboy-style spittin' while you sup*

1   Cut the watermelon in half and lay each half flat-side down on a chopping board. Dear God, please be sure it's not one of those damn chopping boards that's permanently infused with the taste of garlic!
2   Slice the top off and then peel down the sides. You should be left with just the pink flesh (creepy ...) of the watermelon. Chop it up into little cubes.
3   Lash the cubes in a container and pop it in the freezer for a few hours. They don't need to go rock solid, just slushie-esque!
4   Take 'em out, pop 'em in a big jug, blast with a hand blender – all done!

TO SERVE

Looks lovely with a barbecue table spread – I like one big jug decorated with mint and then individual glasses for people to help themselves.

This is also delicious with honeydew melon – prepare it exactly the same way.

TOP TIP

If you want to make it into a cocktail (did someone mention rum?), squeeze the juice of a few limes, dip the rim of your glasses in the lime juice and roll the still-wet edges in some coconut sugar. Fill the glass with the watermelon slushie and add a dash of spiced rum!

Oh, Bollox, I'm a Coeliac – How to Make Good Choices and Deal with the Social Anxiety around Eating Out

If you've recently been diagnosed as a coeliac, or you find that gluten has a really bad effect on you, this section is especially for you. Equally, if you have a gluten-free human in your life, this chunk is well worth a read to help you make their life a little easier, safer and more relaxing.

When I was finally diagnosed it was halfway through my first year of uni in Galway City. Looking back, I could not have been luckier. NUIG is probably the best college in Ireland for looking after coeliacs and the greater Galway area is known to have the highest concentration of coeliacs. I used to make jokes about the gene pool, but who knows?

The college restaurant had loads of gluten-free options, the chefs knew their stuff and the canteen ladies there are probably the most patient, saintly folk on earth. I was off to a good start. As long as I didn't poison myself at breakfast or drunkenly forget what gluten was and eat a burger at Supermacs (yes, that happened once ...) I'd be safe.

As I got more brave/less broke I started venturing out into the culinary scene. Over the years I've lived in Dublin, Galway, Cork and Donegal. Sadly I can't name and shame the places that poisoned me. They would probably sue or something. So what I would say to my fellow newbie and veteran coeliacs is be vigilant! I used to be so awkward about asking for gluten-free stuff that my friends would speak up for me. It took a while for me to put on the big-girl pants. If I had been less of a wuss, I'm sure there would have been fewer poisoning incidents. So here are my top tips for happy eating out:

1

Try different words if the wait staff seem unsure – often coeliac doesn't mean that much to people, but gluten free is more of a buzz phrase. If at that point they say, 'Oh, I don't think there's dairy in that,' be f***king worried. Say it's a bit like a peanut or shellfish allergy and will make you really, really sick. I know it's not technically that bad, of course, but you need to drive home that this is health, not fussiness.

2

Look for places that advertise their gluten-free-ness. Often there is a little sign on their menus – the anti-wheat-looking thing. These are lovely folks who have gone out of their way to make the effort. In fact, when you're there say, 'Cheers, lads, for being so sound.'

3

Get mains without buns. In, for example, an American-style diner, even if their chips are fried with floury things you could still get a chicken breast (essentially a chicken burger without the bun) with something else on the side. It won't be the most exciting meal of your life, but if you don't want to ask your friends/other half to go somewhere else, it's a pretty good option for pub grub too.

4

Look to cuisines that are naturally gluten free. Unless there is a clear indication that they do gluten-free options, silly choices might be: Italian – pizza and pasta, folks; French – floury sauces, pastries, why do it to yourself?; American – often chips are coated in flour or there is wheat rusk in burgers; Chinese – there can be flour in the sauce or some confusion over barley malt extract being in sauces or not (sadly one of my biggest poisoning culprits). The safer bets: Japanese – just ask for tamari soy sauce and stay away from the tempura; Indian – one of the absolute best because so many things are made with rice or chickpea flour instead of wheat; Mexican – with foods based around meat, beans, veg and corn, you will be able to munch away on most of the menu; and finally, and a little surprisingly, Spanish – I lived in Spain for the summer the year after I was diagnosed and, though I always associated it with tasty bread and olive oil, an amazing number of dishes are based around meat, seafood, veg and rice.

5

If the staff are friendly and the chef seems accommodating, sometimes they will do normally floury things gluten free. One of the easiest ways to do this is ordering fish and chips and asking them to pan fry the fish without batter. Lots of restaurants have kindly done this for me – it's extremely tasty, slightly better for you and not a huge bother to anyone!

While I think the mentality is changing in the medical profession in terms of the types of support offered to coeliacs, I don't think anyone ever really talks about the mental aspect of it or the toll it can take on your confidence and self-esteem. I have an uncle who, due to the fear of being poisoned, having had it happen so many times in restaurants, does not eat out any more. Can you imagine that? Will not eat out for the rest of his life. Depressing stuff! For the first few years post-diagnosis – and, to be honest, sometimes still – going out for dinner made me feel anxious too.

What if people think I'm just being fussy?

What if there's nothing I can eat and we have to leave?

What if it's a first date and they think I'm weird?

What if I do get poisoned and need to leave to be ill?

This is not the kind of stuff you want running through your head when you're meant to be having a nice evening out. While I can't guarantee these thoughts will never cross your mind again, I can promise it does get better, you do get more comfortable and I think if you have a light-hearted approach it won't get you down.

I don't make a joke of it, even though I make a joke of most things – your health is serious – but I do have a friendly chat with the waiter. If it's a first date or eating with people I don't know well, I won't make a big song and dance about it – I usually just ask if I can order last. That gives me a little time to talk to the waiter without everyone hanging on my every word.

When you find restaurants that are really good at looking after you, don't be afraid to suggest them when going out – that takes the fear factor out of it for you and puts you at ease for the evening. After all, dinner out is meant to be fun, right?

Finally, the not fun one. Trust your gut. If a place is making you nervous and you think they don't understand, be really clear about what you're worried about. If they don't reassure you? Leave. I remember so many times when I was poisoned and I wish, wish, wish I had done it! Never mind the pain you might feel in the aftermath, there's also the long-term damage it does to your body. You only get one.
Look after it!

Index